"*Prayer Demystified* moves prayer out o ... petition to God and into a powerful relationship encounter with a loving Heavenly Father. It will inspire anyone toward more meaningful prayer experiences, regardless of the present level of your prayer life."

> Norman Wilkie,
> Pastor of Spirit Life Church

"This is a straightforward, practical, delightful guide for those seeking to deepen their relationship with the Father through prayer. Chuck provides doctrinally sound explanations for why we pray, how to create our own prayers, the difference between faith and hope, what we can and cannot expect from prayer. It's a handy guide for lifelong Christians and those who are just beginning their walk with the Lord."

> Tom Culver, Owner Paul Davis Restoration,
> Tulsa OK

"Chuck has masterfully showcased a life of pursuit of the heart of our Heavenly Father. With a heart for his children and a desire to see families restored, Chuck has captured the heart of our Heavenly Father and His desire to restore our relationship with Him through an ongoing relationship based in prayer."

> Dr. Phil Anderson,
> College Professor and Associate Dean,
> Pikes Peak Community College

"Chuck synthesizes the existential truths of living a Spirit-led life in a world, which we all know too well, the prince of darkness can run unchecked. But, as we apply the principles of prayer as explained by Chuck, we can gain victory for our family, our children's children and ourselves. It is heartwarming and inspiring to read the dutiful diligent steps a father took to articulate his faith, to make his life count, and to challenge us to examine our beliefs, faith and prayer-life. Well done."

> Mike Reick

PRAYER DEMYSTIFIED

Uncovering the Secrets to Life-Changing Prayer

Chuck Strohm

PRAYER DEMYSTIFIED
Uncovering the Secrets to Life-Changing Prayer
ISBN: 978-1-939570-48-2
Copyright © 2015 by Chuck Strohm

Published by Word & Spirit Publishing
P.O. Box 701403
Tulsa, OK 74170

Contents

Dedication vii

Foreward ix

Chapter 1: **What is Prayer and Why Do We Pray?** 1

Prayer is How We Talk with God 1

Prayer is Nothing Like Our Life Experience
Says It Is 3

Why Do We Pray? 4

Need-Based Prayer 5

Relational Prayer 6

Understanding the Nature and Character of God 6

Relationship 9

Why Did I Write this Book? 11

A Decision Point in Life 12

Chapter 2: **How to Pray** 17

Chapter 2a: **Spirit vs. Natural World** 19

What is the Prerequisite to Approaching God? 19

We are Flesh and Spirit 20

Natural World 22

Spirit Realm 24

Where the Battle Is 24

Chapter 2b: **How We Approach God in Prayer**............27

Relational Prayer..27

Need-Based Prayer..28

The Lord's Prayer...29

Perseverance...31

Chapter 2c: **Why Doesn't God Just Take Care of My Problems?**...33

Natural and Spiritual Laws..................................34

Chapter 2d: **Faith and Hope**................................39

Hope...39

Faith...40

Examples of Faith vs. Hope................................43

Chapter 2e: **Giving the Word First Place**.............47

Speaking the Word...48

Chapter 2f: **Hearing God**.....................................51

God Primarily Communicates
Three Different Ways:...52

Learning to Hear His Voice..................................54

Expect Opposition..55

Chapter 2g: **Getting Earthly Help**........................57

Healing..57

Provision...59

Chapter 2h: **When do We Receive the Answer to Our Prayer?**......61

What if things don't turn out as you expect?......62

Chapter 2i: **Overview**......67

Steps to ask God to meet a need:......69

Chapter 3: **Word Pictures**......71

The Hand Prayer......71

Faith is Like Gardening – Seedtime and Harvest......73

David and Goliath......76

The Flaming Arrows of the Enemy......79

A Lifelong Dream......80

A Cry for Help......82

Chapter 4: **Prayer Examples**......85

Pray these Prayers Over Your Children......85

Pray These for Yourself and Your Family Members......87

Pray These Scriptures for Healing......89

Chapter 5: **Creating Your Own Prayer**......95

Appendix A: **How to Accept Jesus as Lord**......99

Appendix B: **Scriptures from the Word of God**......103

Building Your Faith......103

Freedom From Fear......106

God's Goodness......108

Healing...112

Marriage..120

Meditating on the Word..125

Peace and Trust...129

Prayer and Faith..135

Protection from Danger...140

Financial Provision..145

Salvation in Jesus..151

Sleep..155

Treatment of Others..157

Dedication

I want to give a special thanks to my daughter Brittany for helping me turn a rough manuscript composed of random thoughts into the book you now hold in your hands. She challenged me every step of the way to become a better writer.

I also want to thank my wife for supporting me through this journey, and for being a Godly partner in life. Your wisdom and insight are invaluable.

Finally, thank you to my mom who taught me about God's love for mankind and His faithfulness to honor His Word. Your steadfast love for our Lord has inspired all of us.

I would like to dedicate this book to my children, their spouses, my grandchildren, and all of their children. Leaving a Christ-centered legacy is, without question, the greatest gift we can leave for both our family and for society.

Deuteronomy 6:4-9[1] commands us to teach our children the Word of the Lord by taking opportunities throughout the day

---

[1] Deuteronomy 6:4-9 (NKJV) Hear, O Israel: The LORD our God, the LORD is one! You shall love the LORD your God with all your heart, with all your soul, and with all your strength. And these words which I command you today shall be in your heart. You shall teach them diligently to your children, and shall talk of them when you sit in your house, when you walk by the way, when you lie down, and when you rise up. You shall bind them as a sign on your hand, and they shall be as frontlets between your eyes. You shall write them on the doorposts of your house and on your gates.

to teach them about God's qualities and faithfulness. As parents, the greatest joy of life is to see our children develop the same passion for God that we have.

Scripture tells us that one of the reasons God chose Abraham to be the father of the Jewish nation was because He knew Abraham would faithfully train Isaac and his entire household in the ways of the Lord. It says in Genesis 18:19 (KJV), "For I know him, that he will command his children and his household after him, and they shall keep the way of the Lord, to do justice and judgment; that the Lord may bring upon Abraham that which he hath spoken of him."

That is why this book is dedicated to my children and the generations that follow because my heart's desire is to pass on what I know about the Word of God, believing that this knowledge will help them impact their world with the Gospel of Jesus Christ. The Gospel is the "Good News" of which we are God's ambassadors to a dying world.

I also dedicate this book to you, the reader, and I pray that you will be blessed by the truths of God's Word in the same way they have impacted my life.

If you don't have a personal relationship with Christ Jesus, I hope that the ideas presented in this book will touch your life and you will come to know Him. It is only through Jesus that our sins can be forgiven; allowing His power to change our lives.

Preface

Life is filled with many challenges that range from horrible life-changing events such as cancer or the death of a child, to less important ones that arise on a daily basis. How we react to these unexpected situations is profoundly affected by our <u>view of God, our understanding of Scripture, and our support network</u>.

The unavoidable fact is this, problems are going to arise, and how we react is directly related to how we have prepared before the problem ever happens.

For thousands of years, people have said that God is "unknow-able and unpredictable," which is code for "He does what He wants" and "why should I even try to understand Him." When we study Scripture, we get a completely different picture of who God is.

The purpose of this book is to explain that we have a loving God who yearns to have a personal one-on-one relationship with humanity. He is interested in our daily lives and cares deeply about every aspect of our lives.

<u>**This book is for new believers**</u> because it answers so many of nagging questions such as "why do bad things happen," "the difference between faith and hope," "how do I pray," "why

doesn't God just take care of my problems," and a whole lot more. It also provides a series of word pictures that explain the concepts of prayer using ideas that we are already familiar with.

It is also a book for lifelong believers because the concepts are timeless. The appendix contains page after page of Scriptures organized by subject matter so that we can easily apply them to the specific areas of life.

My hope is that after reading this book, dynamic and power-filled prayer will be a part of your daily life. The storms of life *will* arise, but by developing your prayer life and confidence in the Word of God, you will be prepared to prevail over every attack of the enemy.

This book is organized like a roadmap.

- First, we talk about *what* is prayer and *why* we pray.

- Second, we talk about *how* to pray.

- Third, we give *word pictures* of prayer.

- Fourth, we give practical *examples* of prayer.

- Finally, the Appendix contains Scriptures that you can pray over your life and your loved ones.

Chapter 1:

What is Prayer and Why Do We Pray?

It is natural for new believers to spend most of their prayer time asking God for help, but as our walk with Him develops, our prayers should move from being need-based to predominantly relational-based.

As we examine all the beauty of this earth, the intricacies of our human body, the vastness of the universe, all of these pale in comparison with the awesomeness of having a personal relationship with our Creator. Prayer is the primary way we experience this wonderful relationship.

Prayer is How We Talk with God

If you are like me, I do most of the talking during my prayer times, meaning that I take very little time to listen for God to speak. Ponder this statement for a moment. We have an audience with the Creator of the universe and *we do most of the talking*.

Rather than "talking *to* God," prayer should really be "talking *with* Him." This is a crucial difference because we often talk *to* God, but rarely take time to listen for a response. Learning to hear His voice becomes a lifelong journey that changes every aspect of our lives.

As we consider the idea of prayer, let's examine it from two different viewpoints:

> The first viewpoint is the **relational-aspect** of prayer. This is the part where we talk with God as our Heavenly Father, just as we talk with a spouse or family member. By spending time each day telling Him how much we love Him while being grateful for all the blessings in our lives, we keep a healthy perspective on life while maintaining a strong relationship with Him. Many of the Psalms are such prayers.

> The second viewpoint is the **request-aspect** of prayer. This is the part of prayer where we come to God and ask Him to meet our daily needs as well as any major needs we may have. It is also the part of prayer when we cry out to God to help deliver us during temptation to sin.

It is natural for new believers to spend most of their prayer time asking God for help, but as our walk with Him develops, our prayers should move from being need-based to predominantly relational-based. That is where the true joy of being a Christian becomes evident because we are no longer asking God to deliver us from one trial after another. Instead, we are coming to Him to express the joys of the Christian life.

This book is not a magic set of instructions to get whatever we want. The ideas presented are rooted in the belief that God's Will is knowable through His Word, and that He honors His Word when we pray in agreement with it.

The focus on this book is about relationship, God's character, Biblical truths, personal responsibility, and the fact that we are Christ's ambassadors here on the earth. By developing an understanding of these ideas, we see that God's desire is for us to live a life of victory here on the earth so that we can touch the lives of non-believers and lead them to a personal relationship with Jesus Christ.

Prayer is Nothing Like Our Life Experience Says It Is

At some point in our own human experience, we will need to choose whether we allow the experiences of this world or the Word of God to define absolute truth.

In order to explain the statement that prayer is not like our human experience, let's examine the idea of *normal* and how our personal experience influences this.

How many of us have traveled to another part of this wonderful country only to find out that we have completely failed to pack the right clothes even though we knew better. A subconscious part of our brain told us that the weather where we were going could not be *that* different from where we live.

My daughter experienced this exact scenario when she went hiking with a group of friends in the mountains of California. The weather was sunny and beautiful at the foothills, and, even though there were signs warning of cold temperatures on the mountain, it was impossible for them to grasp how cold it would actually be. The weather at the base of the mountain defined their _normal_, resulting in a chilly hiking trip because they didn't have enough cold weather clothing.

This idea is true whether we are talking about weather, finances, or any other part of life because the longer we spend in a particular situation, the more we allow it to define what we consider _normal._

This idea impacts the way we view God because we have a tendency to define God within the confines of our own personal experience, rather than through the truths of Scripture. Because of this, many people have an idea of God and prayer that is totally inconsistent with the Word.

As we journey through the pages of Scripture, our goal is to take a biblical look at prayer and explore the idea that what we consider _normal_, based upon our human experience, does not necessarily line up with the Word of God. We learn we are surrounded by a supernatural world, which has greater impact on our life than any of us really understands.

Why Do We Pray?

We pray because we either **have a need** in our life or we want to experience our **relationship with God.**

Let's delve into these ideas a little deeper and see if we can understand each one a little more.

Need-Based Prayer

God gave us His Word so that we can learn about His character and nature, which helps us understand that He wants us to live a life of victory while living on this earth.

When my kids ask me for something, they trust that I have the ability to give them what they are asking for. The same concept applies to prayer because we must come to a point where we trust that God is _able_ to answer our request; otherwise there is no point in asking Him. Simply put, if we don't believe that God has the ability to answer our request, then _why pray_?

For many people, _prayer is something that you just do_ out of habit or ritual, but there is no power behind it. If in a serious condition, people often pray to help deal with emotional trauma, but there is no expectancy that God will actually answer the request. Prayer is seen more as a placebo than as a solution. As someone who prays for a lot of people, I know when people view prayer this way because the first thing out of their mouths are words of unbelief that contradict the prayer.

God gave us His Word so we can learn about His character and nature, which helps us understand that He wants us to live a life of victory while living on this earth. His Word is filled with wisdom and practical truths, and if we apply them to our lives, we can live in victory over the struggles of this world.

> That is why a regular time of Bible study is important. Unless we take time to study God's Word, we will never really learn about God's many promises and how to develop the faith necessary to bring these promises into our lives!

Relational Prayer

Just as it is impossible to maintain a healthy relationship with our spouse if we don't talk, it is impossible to maintain a relationship with God if we ignore Him throughout the day. We can talk and listen just like we do with a spouse or close friend.

As our walk with God develops, our prayers will naturally turn from being prayers of need to being prayers of fellowship, which is one of the most wonderful parts of being a believer in Christ.

Understanding the Nature and Character of God

God is nothing like the world says He is. He is a loving Father who sent His Son to pay the price for the sins of mankind, and then sent His Spirit to live inside all those who believe. His desire is for us to live a life of daily fellowship with Him.

Before we can feel safe trusting God and putting every aspect of our life in His hands, we have to learn what He is like and that He cares about us.

It is very common for people to have a dysfunctional perception of God because of daily human interactions or baggage from our parental relationships. Often, we have an opinion of God based on our own experiences only to find out that it does not line up with Scripture.

Nothing drives this point home more than listening to the news during a natural disaster as we hear these "acts of Satan" being called "acts of God." Rather than viewing Him as a loving Father, the world views Him as a judgmental God waiting for the first opportunity to teach us a lesson.

One last thing that often affects our perception of Him is the feeling that He let us down when things don't turn out like we wanted. An entire book could be written on this subject, but Scripture is clear that **God never lets us down**. The Word tells us over and over that <u>God's Word does not return void</u>[2], that <u>He watches over His Word to perform it</u>[3] and <u>all the promises of God are yes and amen in Christ Jesus.</u>[4] So if we are praying in agreement with the Word and still not seeing our prayers answered, then it's time to ask..."What could we be doing wrong?"

There are a variety of things that can hinder our prayer life including:

- Not praying in agreement with the Word.
- Trusting in man for the answer rather than God. (God may use a person to provide the answer, but the ultimate answer comes from Him.)
- Pride.
- Unforgiveness.
- Strife, particularly with your spouse.[5]
- Unwillingness to deal with sin.
- Refusing to change something that would lead to a natural solution. In effect, expecting God to solve a problem that should clearly be solved in the natural.[6]

---

[2] Isaiah 55:11 (KJV) "So shall my word be that goeth forth out of my mouth: it shall not return unto me void, but it shall accomplish that which I please, and it shall prosper in the thing whereto I sent it."

[3] Jeremiah 1:12 (AMP) "Then said the Lord to me, You have seen well, for I am alert *and* active, watching over My word to perform it."

[4] 2 Corinthians 1:20 (NIV) "For no matter how many promises God has made, they are "Yes" in Christ. And so through him the "Amen" is spoken by us to the glory of God."

[5] 1 Peter 3:7 (NIV) "Husbands, in the same way be considerate as you live with your wives, and treat them with respect as the weaker partner and as heirs with you of the gracious gift of life, so that nothing will hinder your prayers."

[6] 1 Timothy 5:23 (NIV) "Stop drinking only water, and use a little wine because of your stomach and your frequent illnesses."

Hebrews 4:14-16[7] is a great example of how God's character is quite different than the world expects, as He tells us to <u>run toward Him</u> during the moment of temptation, which is exactly the opposite of what we would expect Him to say. When we are tempted, our human emotions tell us to do what Adam and Eve did when they sinned and hid from God. The writer of Hebrews explains that when we are at the door of sinning, God says to "come boldly unto the throne of grace, that we may obtain mercy, and find grace to help in time of need." <u>If God tells us to approach Him with boldness at the moment of temptation, how much more does He want us to approach Him when we have a genuine need in our life!</u>

John 10:10 clearly states that *Jesus came that we may have life, and have it more abundantly.*[8]

We serve a loving Father who sent His Son to pay the price for the sins of mankind, and then sent His Spirit to live inside all those who believe. Just like King David, Abraham, or the Apostle John, God's desire is for us to live a life of daily fellowship with Him. Developing an understanding of this relationship is key to living a victorious life in Christ.

---

[7] Hebrews 4:14-16 (NKJV) " Seeing then that we have a great High Priest who has passed through the heavens, Jesus the Son of God, let us hold fast *our* confession. For we do not have a High Priest who cannot sympathize with our weaknesses, but was in all *points* tempted as *we are, yet* without sin. Let us therefore come boldly to the throne of grace, that we may obtain mercy and find grace to help in time of need.

[8] John 10:10 (NKJV) " The thief does not come except to steal, and to kill, and to destroy. I have come that they may have life, and that they may have *it* more abundantly."

Relationship

God created mankind in His image so that we could fellowship with Him. Man's sin changed all that. He gives His Spirit to all who accept Jesus as Lord so that we can have this fellowship once again.

The idea of relationship is important in every aspect of life. Whether in family, church, or business, our relationship with people has a major influence on our ability to speak into their lives.

This idea is quite simple to understand if we look at it from a parent/child relationship. Let's consider two different scenarios to make this point more apparent.

First, let's consider scenario one where the parent has two children who are both great kids. Because the parent has a good relationship with both of them, doesn't it make sense that the parent will bless and help both children as much as possible? What's more, a really great parent will find ways to uniquely bless each child in ways that express love and appreciation based upon that child's personality.

Now, let's consider scenario two where the same parent has two children, except that one is doing something that is destructive or rebellious. Should a good parent treat both kids the same? Of course not!

Relationship determines the level of blessing and influence in life, and if a parent continues to treat a rebellious child the same as a child who shows respect, then two things occur. First, the respectful child gets discouraged and loses hope in the value of doing what's right. Second, the parent is subconsciously reinforcing the idea that rebellion is OK. Proverbs tells us that

rebellion is destructive, contagious, and should not be encouraged. Generally, rebellious children do not even understand
that they themselves are withholding the blessing they so
desperately seek. Simply stated, the parent wants to bless this
child but cannot.

Let's look at this from the spiritual standpoint. The Bible is
filled with verse after verse telling us how much God desires to
bless us. Romans 8:31-32[9] is so pertinent because it tells us that
God, who sacrificed his own Son for the sins of the world, also
wants to "graciously give us all things." God's desire to bless us
just like we want to bless our children shows the heart of a
loving Father.

> Unfortunately, by living a life that is not much different
> than the non-Christian world, so many Christians limit
> the ability of God to work in their lives.

As believers, our goal should be to seek out the heart of God
through regular Bible study and church attendance, and then to
ask the Holy Spirit to help us live a life that pleases Him.

By living a life that is pleasing to God, something amazing
happens. Our desire for things that are not important begins to
fade as our life is shaped by the Word of God and His Holy Spirit.
This profoundly affects not only our choices, but changes our
inner desires so that we no longer want to live a life of mediocrity.

---

[9] Romans 8:31-32 (NIV) " What, then, shall we say in response to these things?
If God is for us, who can be against us? He who did not spare his own Son,
but gave him up for us all—how will he not also, along with him, graciously
give us all things?"

Why Did I Write this Book?

I wrote this book because the principles I have learned about God's love and faithfulness have been so earth shattering that I felt compelled to share them. <u>More importantly, I know that if I cannot pass these ideas on to my children then I have failed, because the greatest responsibility a parent has is passing their love for God on to the generations that follow.</u>

After striving for many years to be successful, I am learning to understand what it means to rest in the peace of God by committing my steps to Him and trusting that He is faithful to walk with me through the remainder of life's journey.[10]

The concepts in this book were birthed out of the pain of loss, followed by a time of digging into God's Word to find specific promises related to my situation, after which I battled through the circumstances of life learning to apply these biblical promises to each struggle that came up. <u>Prayer was a key component during every step.</u>

The culmination of this process that has lasted almost twenty years, is nothing short of extraordinary. I have learned that God is faithful to His Word, and it brings Him great joy when His children desire a daily relationship with Him.

---

[10] John 17:3 (NIV) "Now this is eternal life: that they know you, the only true God, and Jesus Christ, whom you have sent."

A Decision Point in Life

When I was about thirty years old, I came to a decision point in life that forced me to choose whether I would live a life of mediocrity or whether I would trust God in a way that I never thought possible. In effect, I had to decide if I was going to put my trust in God's Word, or whether I was going to put my faith in the world that surrounded me.

Let's rewind many years to see what brought me to this point. I grew up in a small local church with a mom who had a passionate love for God and a dad who was a good moral man but did not believe in Christ until later in life. I loved going to church every time the doors were open.

While the church I grew up in had many people with a wonderful love for Jesus, there was not a lot of teaching on the deeper concepts of God. Despite this fact, my knowledge of God exploded during my teen years, and one night in youth group I experienced the touch of God. After talking to my pastor, who did not know how to answer my questions, he directed me to my mom. She explained that what I sensed was the voice of the Holy Spirit, and my life was changed forever that very night when I received His infilling.

My desire to learn about God grew, and I began having a regular Bible study and prayer time that focused me like a laser and filled my heart with a desire to please God. I was careful to "guard my heart" as Proverbs 4:23[11] says.

---

[11] Proverbs 4:23 (NKJV) "Keep your heart with all diligence, For out of it *spring* the issues of life."

My life took a turn of direction when I left for college, became physically involved with my girlfriend, and found myself married at the age of twenty-one. We had two wonderful children together and did our best to make things work but, looking back, it is clear that I was completely unprepared for marriage and the work that it requires to be successful. Parenthood came naturally to me, and I was a great daddy, but being a great husband was another matter. Not being a better husband is one of my greatest life failures, and despite our efforts, things ended in divorce eight years later.

If you know anyone at work who fills their walls with their kid's artwork, that was me—because I loved spending time with them. They meant everything to me, and the idea of not seeing them and tucking them into bed every night was devastating. Making matters worse was the idea that another man would spend time with them and influence their lives.

While going through the divorce proceedings, I was also feeling the disappointment of an unfulfilled career that was only six years old, and when I thought things could not get any worse, my ex-wife moved our kids to another city about an hour and twenty minutes away.

This was more than I could take, and I still remember kneeling at the side of my bed and weeping for what seemed an eternity. While in a complete state of brokenness, I heard a small voice inside me quote Psalm 126:5-6 (KJV) which says, "They that sow in tears shall reap in joy. He that goeth forth and weepeth, bearing precious seed, shall doubtless come again with rejoicing, bringing his sheaves with him." At some point in my past, I had heard that Scripture, and the Holy Spirit brought it back to my memory. At that crucial moment, this verse brought me tremendous comfort because I was sowing more tears than I ever had.

<u>At that moment, I realized that something needed to change</u> because, up to that point, I had been making decisions out of anger, frustration, and bitterness toward my ex-wife. I knew that God could not bless my life while I held on to unforgiveness.

Over the following days, I took my worn Thompson Chain Reference Bible and wrote down every promise of God that applied to my life. It started out as a couple of pages and soon grew into page after page of Scriptures. I would speak those promises over my family every morning and evening. It took a long time, but eventually I got to the point where I could speak those blessings over the life of my ex-wife as well.

Things did not change right away, but the first verse I stood on was Deuteronomy 20:1-4 (NIV): "When you go to war against your enemies and see horses and chariots and an army greater than yours, do not be afraid of them, because the LORD your God, who brought you up out of Egypt, will be with you. When you are about to go into battle, the priest shall come forward and address the army. He shall say: 'Hear, O Israel, today you are going into battle against your enemies. Do not be fainthearted or afraid; do not be terrified or give way to panic before them. For the LORD your God is the one who goes with you to fight for you against your enemies to give you victory.'" I stood on this verse because I felt like an undefeatable army of the court system, judge, and lawyers were waging a war against my relationship with my kids. The weight of carrying this was overwhelming, and it was time to allow my Lord to carry it.

It became obvious that my kids were not going to come back home through my own efforts, and God was going to have to intervene. When I started speaking Deuteronomy 20, it felt as though heaven and earth moved when I spoke His Word. I knew that things were going to change.

The other unexpected thing that happened was a sense of incredible peace as I spoke His Word. I *knew* that God was going to bring my children back to me because I was praying in accordance with His Word. Malachi 4:5-6[12] talks about God turning the hearts of the fathers toward their children and the hearts of the children toward the fathers. He knew that my heart had been toward my children long before they were ever born. Every time fear would enter my heart, I would speak Deuteronomy 20:1-4, and great peace would come over me. It did not happen overnight, but my kids eventually moved back home. What a wonderful day it was!

I continued to add promises to my tattered list and after twelve or thirteen pages, I realized it made sense to organize it by subject. It took several nights of working until two or three in the morning, but I transcribed all the hand written pages into the following series of promises from God.

---

[12] Malachi 4:5-6 (NKJV) " Behold, I will send you Elijah the prophet before the coming of the great and dreadful day of the LORD. And he will turn the hearts of the fathers to the children, and the hearts of the children to their fathers, lest I come and strike the earth with a curse."

- Building Your Faith
- Peace and Trust
- Meditating on the Word
- Prayer and Faith
- Marriage
- Protection from Danger
- Healing
- Provision
- Freedom from Fear
- Salvation
- God's Goodness
- Sleep

It has been almost twenty years now, and my walk with the Lord is more stable and solid than ever. The journey has not been easy, but through each challenge and victory, my understanding of God's faithfulness has been strengthened.

What's more, **by committing Scripture to memory, my life has been transformed**. I am no longer the man I was twenty, ten, five, or even one year ago.

My driven personality no longer yearns for earthly success; rather it asks "what can I do to point others to you, Lord?" Over the last couple of years, the idea of eternal riches has begun to shape my life in a way that I never expected. When my time comes to pass from this earthly realm into eternity, I want to hear that I made a good use of my gifts and talents while here on the earth. I also want to hear that I did a great job training my children and grandchildren to know Him.

Chapter 2:

How to Pray

The following sub-chapters walk through the process of how to pray and try to answer many of the questions believers have regarding prayer.

The last sub-chapter is a summary which takes all of these ideas and pulls them together into a simple list that we can put on the refrigerator or wall at work to remind ourselves of these biblical principles.

Chapter 2 is Broken Into the Following Sections:

2a. Spirit vs. Natural World

2b. How We Approach God in Prayer

2c. Why Doesn't God Just Take Care of My Problems

2d. Faith and Hope

2e. Giving the Word First Place

2f. Hearing God

2g. Getting Earthly Help

2h. When do We Receive the Answer to Our Prayer

2i. Overview

Chapter 2a

Spirit vs. Natural World

What is the Prerequisite to Approaching God?

John 3:16 (KJV) "For God so loved the world, that he gave his only begotten Son, that whosoever believeth in him should not perish, but have everlasting life."

In the Beginning – God's Perfect Plan

God's plan was to have an intimate face-to-face relationship with mankind, which is how things were before Adam and Eve sinned. Genesis 1:26 tells us, "Then God said, 'Let us make mankind in our image, in our likeness.'" I believe the reason God created man in His image and likeness was so that He could have a relationship with beings that could choose to have a relationship with Him.

> After God created mankind, but before Adam fell, they enjoyed such an intimate relationship that they would walk in the cool of the day[13] just like friends might sit around a table enjoying a cup of coffee.

---

[13] Genesis 3:8 (NKJV) "And they heard the voice of the LORD God walking in the garden in the cool of the day, and Adam and his wife hid themselves from the presence of the Lord God amongst the trees of the garden."

Sin and Separation from God

After the fall of mankind, everything changed. Adam was banished from Eden and his face-to-face walks with God came to an abrupt end. The intimate relationship mankind had with our creator was gone and the curse of sin and death came on the earth.

God loved mankind so much, He sent His Son to die on a cross and pay the price for the sin of mankind so that we could be restored to Him.

The one prerequisite to approaching God is salvation in Jesus Christ. <u>Unless we accept God's free gift of salvation, we do not have any spiritual basis to approach Him with our requests.</u>

> If you want to know more about trusting Jesus as Lord, there is a section in the Appendix titled "How to Accept Jesus as Lord."

We are Flesh and Spirit

The battles we fight are not earthly; they are spiritual. Our spirit man is the part of us that wages war in this conflict.

When God created mankind in His image, He made us with three distinct parts:

- Spirit man – this is our innermost part that will live forever.
- Soul – this is our mind, will, and emotions.
- Body – this is our physical body that requires daily physical maintenance.

When we accept Jesus as Lord and Savior, Colossians 1:13-14[14] tells us that the Father <u>translates</u> us from the <u>kingdom of darkness</u> into the <u>kingdom of His dear Son</u>.

The question to ask is, "What part of us gets translated?"

In order to answer this, let's look at Romans 8:9-10 (NIV) which says "You, however, are not in the realm of the flesh but are in the realm of the Spirit, if indeed the Spirit of God lives in you." Romans 8:16 (NIV) also says, "The Spirit himself testifies with our spirit that we are God's children." <u>It is clear from these verses that our spirit is the part of us that is translated (renewed) when we accept Jesus as Lord.</u>

The word "flesh" is used through these verses, and it refers to our physical body and soul. Romans 8:1-17 and Galatians 5:16-26 provide detailed differences between the flesh and spirit while explaining that the flesh cannot please God because it is part of this earthly kingdom.

Even after we become believers in Christ, our flesh still wants to sin because it was not transformed. It is our transformed spirit that gives us strength to overcome the lust of the flesh[15] by living

---

[14] Colossians 1:13-14 (AMP) " [The Father] has delivered *and* drawn us to Himself out of the control *and* the dominion of darkness and has transferred us into the kingdom of the Son of His love, in Whom we have our redemption *through His blood*, [which means] the forgiveness of our sins."

[15] 1 John 2:16 (NKJV) " For all that *is* in the world—the lust of the flesh, the lust of the eyes, and the pride of life—is not of the Father but is of the world."

a life according to the spirit.[16] We do this by committing God's Word to memory, staying in prayer, spending time with other believers, attending church, and sharing God's message of salvation with others.

Our flesh and spirit struggle against each other, one wanting to sin and the other desiring to live a life pleasing to God. The one that wins is the one you spend the most time developing.

I find it easiest to conceptualize these ideas by recognizing that we live in two different worlds at the same time. One is the *Natural World,* and the other is the *Spirit Realm.*

Natural World

The natural world is the earthly kingdom we live in. We eat, go to work, have children, and eventually die a physical death. This is the world that is full of death, decay, strife, and sin. The world became this way as a result of Adam's choice to obey Satan by eating from the Tree of the Knowledge of Good and Evil.

Even after becoming a Christian, our flesh still resides in this natural world where Satan has authority and dominion.

In order to understand the idea of authority, let's take a look at the contract God made with man when He originally created him.

---

[16] Galatians 5:16 (NIV) "So I say, walk by the Spirit, and you will not gratify the desires of the flesh."

Genesis 1:26 (NIV) says, "Then God said, 'Let us make man-kind in our image, in our likeness, so that they may <u>rule</u> over the fish in the sea and the birds in the sky, over the livestock and all the wild animals, and <u>over all</u> the creatures that move along the ground.'" And Genesis 1:28-30 (NIV) says, " God blessed them and said to them, 'Be fruitful and increase in number; fill the earth and <u>subdue it</u>. <u>Rule</u> over the fish in the sea and the birds in the sky and <u>over every living creature</u> that moves on the ground.' Then God said, '<u>I give you</u> every seed-bearing plant on the face of the <u>whole</u> earth and every tree that has fruit with seed in it. <u>They will be yours</u> for food. And to <u>all</u> the beasts of the earth and <u>all</u> the birds in the sky and <u>all</u> the creatures that move along the ground—<u>everything that has the breath of life in it</u>—I give <u>every</u> green plant for food.' And it was so."

> It is clear from these verses that God told Adam to rule over the whole earth and subdue it. When God created the earth, He still had authority. But when He put Adam in charge, He turned that authority over to Adam.

When Adam chose to eat from the Tree of the Knowledge of Good and Evil, he chose to obey Satan rather than God, result-ing in a legal transaction taking place. Because God had given Adam authority over the earth, <u>Adam willingly turned this authority over to Satan, meaning that Adam, and indirectly God, lost the legal authority over the earth.</u>

It is very important to understand that God chooses to be bound by the decision He made with Adam, which is why we see all the terrible things going on around us.

The good news is the fact that God exists outside our time domain, so He saw all of this before the world was ever created and provided a solution that would result in the defeat of Satan.

Spirit Realm

The spirit realm is the unseen world that influences our lives every moment of every day. This is divided into godly forces and those opposed to God (forces of darkness).

This is the world where our translated spirit lives. Ephesians 2:6 even explains that we are seated with Christ Jesus in heavenly places.[17] What an amazing thought!

In contrast to godly forces, the forces of darkness (evil spirits) bring sickness and disease, and actively work through people to cause problems. Every time they look at a believer in Jesus, they feel animosity because His Spirit dwells in us.

God is in control in the spirit realm.

Where the Battle Is

Ephesians 6:12 (NIV) says, "For our struggle is not against flesh and blood, but against the rulers, against the authorities, against the powers of this dark world and against the spiritual forces of evil in the heavenly realms."

---

[17] Ephesians 2:6 (NKJV) "and raised *us* up together, and made *us* sit together in the heavenly *places* in Christ Jesus,"

Our battles may be fought here on this earth, but the real battle is spiritual.

Once we realize that spiritual forces of darkness are the real enemy, it becomes clear that the only way to fight them is in the spirit realm[18] by quoting God's Word just like Jesus did.[19]

In order for Jesus to take on the sins of mankind, He had to be tempted in every possible way that we could be tempted.[20] After fasting for forty days, Matthew 4:1-11 explains that the Lord did not argue or try to negotiate with Satan when faced with each of the three temptations. He responded by quoting the Word.

Second Corinthians 10:3-5 (NIV) tells us that, "For though we live in the world, we do not wage war as the world does. The weapons we fight with are not the weapons of the world. On the contrary, they have divine power to demolish strongholds. We demolish arguments and every pretension that sets itself up against the knowledge of God, and we take captive every thought to make it obedient to Christ."

---

[18] Ephesians 6:13 (NIV) " Therefore put on the full armor of God, so that when the day of evil comes, you may be able to stand your ground, and after you have done everything, to stand."

[19] Matthew 4:4, 7, & 10 (NKJV) "But He answered and said, It is written, Man shall not live by bread alone, but by every word that proceeds from the mouth of God. It is written again, You shall not tempt the Lord your God. Then Jesus said to him, Away with you, Satan! For it is written, You shall worship the Lord your God, and Him only you shall serve."

[20] Hebrews 4:15 (NKJV) "For we do not have a High Priest who cannot sympathize with our weaknesses, but was in all *points* tempted as *we are, yet* without sin."

Even though the enemy tries to harm us in this natural world, we overcome him by speaking the Word of God.

As we speak God's Word, something amazing happens. The natural world starts to change so that it is in agreement with the spoken Word of God. This may not happen immediately, but if we don't give up, God's Word will overcome.

At some point in our own human experience, we will need to choose whether we allow the experiences of this world or the Word of God to define absolute truth.

Chapter 2b:

How We Approach God in Prayer

When we approach God, our prayers generally fall into two categories. These include relational prayer and need-based prayer.

Relational Prayer

If people are married and have a healthy marriage, they communicate with their spouses from the early moments of the day until they kiss each other goodnight. If they go throughout their day without saying anything, then the obvious question arises, "What is wrong?" Yet that is exactly what many believers do with God! They go throughout their day without talking with Him.

> When Jesus went to Heaven and sat down at the right hand of the Father, the Bible tells us that He sent the Holy Spirit to dwell inside of those who believe.[21] Our

---

[21] John 16:7 (NIV) "But very truly I tell you, it is for your good that I am going away. Unless I go away, the Advocate will not come to you; but if I go, I will send him to you."

body is called the "temple of the Holy Spirit,"[22] meaning God literally resides within us.

Just as it is impossible to maintain a healthy relationship with our spouse if we don't talk, it is impossible to maintain a relationship with God if we ignore Him all day. Our prayers don't need to be long and drawn out. Rather, we can just <u>talk and listen</u> like we do with a spouse or close friend.

Relational prayer is one of the most wonderful parts of being a believer in Christ. When I wake up, I often find that my spirit is praising God before I am really coherent. This is particularly true if I was listening to praise music the evening before. During the day, I speak to Him when I need wisdom or just to say thank you. When one of my children is having difficulties, the Holy Spirit often impresses on my heart the need to pray for them. To know that the Creator of the universe loves and wants to have a relationship with us is almost overwhelming to think about!

While we can't walk with Him in the cool of the day back in Eden, we can walk with Him every moment of every day because He resides within us.

Need-Based Prayer

There is a major difference between relational prayer and need-based prayer. Consider the example of a son or a daughter

---

[22] 1 Corinthians 6:19-20 (NIV) " Do you not know that your bodies are temples of the Holy Spirit, who is in you, whom you have received from God? You are not your own; you were bought at a price. Therefore honor God with your bodies."

needing to ask a parent to borrow money for a car. We know that the son or daughter has to approach the parent differently if they need to borrow a large, rather than a small, amount of money. First, they determine if the parent can even afford what is being asked for, and then they prepare to answer all the tough questions the parent may ask. Finally, they develop an attitude of humility so that the request can be presented in an appropriate manner, because humility always engenders favor.

The Lord's Prayer

Approaching God follows a similar pattern. In Matthew 6:9-15, we find the disciples asking the Lord to teach them how to pray. He responded with what has been called "The Lord's Prayer," a beautiful example of how to approach God when we have a need.

Matthew 6:9-15 (NASB) says, "Pray, then, in this way: 'Our Father who is in heaven, Hallowed be Your name. Your kingdom come. Your will be done, on earth as it is in heaven. Give us this day our daily bread. And forgive us our debts, as we also have forgiven our debtors.

And do not lead us into temptation, but deliver us from evil. [For Yours is the kingdom and the power and the glory forever. Amen.]' For if you forgive others for their transgressions, your heavenly Father will also forgive you. But if you do not forgive others, then your Father will not forgive your transgressions."

Verses 9-10 tell us that the first thing we do is praise God and ask that His will be done on this earth as it is in Heaven. Two things happen when we do this: First, when we approach God in an attitude of worship, we show that we respect and love Him. Second, by asking that His will be done and in our lives, we are releasing our earthly legal authority so that He has the right to work His will in our situation. Remember, Adam gave Satan authority over this natural world where we live and **by our asking, we are opening the door so that God can step in and change things in our lives. That is why we must ask.**

Verse 11 tells us that God is our source for "our daily bread" or any need we may have. While our job may be the way we receive a paycheck, the true source of our income is God. He is our healer, provider, deliverer, and savior. By understanding this concept, tithing becomes something we truly take joy in because we recognize what an honor it is to say "thank you" to the one who provides. It is amazing how God blesses the remaining 90% when we tithe.

Verses 12, 14-15 remind us to forgive. God tells us that if we choose to hold on to unforgiveness, He will be unable to forgive us. Yet if we forgive, God forgives us. The irony is that by holding on to unforgiveness, the person we are bitter toward is rarely harmed. Choosing to forgive when we've been wronged prevents the enemy from causing bitterness to grow in us. It also prevents health and emotional issues that cause us to get sick and impact our lives in more ways than we will ever know.

Forgiveness, is a spiritual force that requires the power of the Holy Spirit to help us overcome the power of bitterness and live a life pleasing to God.

<u>Verse 13</u> instructs us to ask God to deliver us from evil. James
1:13[23] makes it very clear that God is not the one who tempts us,
but He is certainly the one who delivers us. Hebrews 4:16[24] tells
us that when we are tempted, we should come boldly before the
throne of grace to find mercy and favor to help in time of need.

Perseverance

Because Luke was a doctor, we are provided with a unique
perspective of the Lord's Prayer that is not found in Matthew
and Mark.

Luke 11:5-13 (NIV) adds, " Then Jesus said to them, 'Suppose
you have a friend, and you go to him at midnight and say,
"Friend, lend me three loaves of bread; a friend of mine on a
journey has come to me, and I have no food to offer him." And
suppose the one inside answers, "Don't bother me. The door is
already locked, and my children and I are in bed. I can't get up
and give you anything." I tell you, even though he will not get
up and give you the bread because of friendship, yet because of
your shameless audacity he will surely get up and give you as
much as you need. So I say to you: Ask and it will be given to
you; seek and you will find; knock and the door will be opened
to you. For everyone who asks receives; the one who seeks finds;
and to the one who knocks, the door will be opened. Which of
you fathers, if your son asks for a fish, will give him a snake

---

[23] James 1:13 (NIV) "When tempted, no one should say, 'God is tempting me.'
For God cannot be tempted by evil, nor does he tempt anyone."

[24] Hebrews 4:16 (NIV) "Let us then approach God's throne of grace with confidence, so that we may receive mercy and find grace to help us in our time of need."

instead? Or if he asks for an egg, will give him a scorpion? If you then, though you are evil, know how to give good gifts to your children, how much more will your Father in heaven give the Holy Spirit to those who ask him!'"

Luke's account contrasts our relationship with God against human relationships and explains that He is trustworthy and faithful when we ask Him for help.

He also wants us to be diligent when we ask. In effect, find out what God's Word says and then dig our heels in. Moreover, 1 John 5: 14-15[25] tells us that if we ask according to His will, He hears us; and if He hears us, then we have the request that we made of Him.

---

[25] 1 John 5:14-15 (NIV) " This is the confidence we have in approaching God: that if we ask anything according to his will, he hears us. And if we know that he hears us—whatever we ask—we know that we have what we asked of him."

Chapter 2c:

Why Doesn't God Just Take Care of My Problems?

In order for God to help us, we need to ask for help and then release control, knowing that He has our best interests in mind.

> The question we all ask is this: "If God knows I have a need, why doesn't He just take care of it? After all; isn't He all-powerful and all-knowing?"

If a parent sees a child having a problem with their car, most loving parents will take care of this problem, either by offering to pay for the repair or just fixing it. We don't have to wait for our child to ask for help – we just do it!

For instance, if we see that one of our children has a tire that is ready to have a blowout, a loving parent will immediately have the tire replaced. We fix the problem without our child having to ask.

Most people feel that if we take care of our kids needs without them asking, shouldn't God do the same for us? After all, the

God who created this earthly kingdom is far better equipped to help us than we are to help our children.

Even though our earthly experience tells us that God should help us without asking, Scripture explains that for God to help us, we must ask.

Romans 8:32 (NIV) says, "He who did not spare his own Son, but gave him up for us all – how will he not also, along with him graciously give us all things?"

If God doesn't just step in and help when Romans 8:32 tells us that He wants to, then this means there must be something that prevents Him from doing so. After all, is the God who sacrificed His own Son for the sins of the world willing to withhold the help we obviously need, or is there a reason that prevents Him from stepping in on His own initiative?

Natural and Spiritual Laws

In order to answer this question, let's take another look at the natural and spiritual laws God established when He created the universe.

The natural laws govern how the atom works, how our cells operate, and what type of math is required to send a man to the moon. Several fields of study devoted to understanding these laws include astronomy, biology, chemistry, physics, math, medicine, etc.

The spiritual laws govern how the spirit and earthly worlds interact and how much influence spiritual forces have in our earthly kingdom.

God <u>chooses</u> to be bound by the spiritual laws He established because <u>it means that every other spiritual being
must be bound by the very same laws.</u>

Let's fast forward through the first five days of creation and stop
on day six when Genesis 1:31 (NIV) tells us, "God saw all that
he had made, and it was <u>very good</u>. And there was evening, and
there was morning—the sixth day." Now, let's turn to Colossians
1:13 (NIV), where we are told, "For he has rescued us from the
<u>dominion of darkness</u> and brought us into the kingdom of the
Son he loves."

How did something that was "very good" become a
"dominion of darkness?"

In order to understand this, we need to understand a little about
the legal system and the contract God made with mankind
through Adam.

If a judge were faced with hearing a case that involved one of his
own children, he (or she) would have to recuse himself because
of the conflict it would create. Nevertheless, if it did happen, the
judge would be obligated to carry out the law even if it meant
sending one of his own children to prison.

Let's re-examine Genesis 1:26 (NIV), which says, "Then God
said, 'Let us make mankind in our image, in our likeness, so that
they may <u>rule</u> over the fish in the sea and the birds in the sky,
over the livestock and all the wild animals, and <u>over all</u> the creatures that move along the ground.'" And Genesis 1:28-30
(NIV) says, " God blessed them and said to them, 'Be fruitful
and increase in number; fill the earth and <u>subdue it</u>. <u>Rule</u> over

the fish in the sea and the birds in the sky and <u>over every living creature</u> that moves on the ground.' Then God said, "<u>I give you</u> every seed-bearing plant on the face of the <u>whole</u> earth and every tree that has fruit with seed in it. <u>They will be yours</u> for food. And to <u>all</u> the beasts of the earth and <u>all</u> the birds in the sky and <u>all</u> the creatures that move along the ground—<u>everything that has the breath of life in it</u>—I give <u>every</u> green plant for food.' And it was so." **It is clear from these verses that God told Adam to <u>rule over the whole earth and subdue it.</u>**

> When Adam chose to obey Satan rather than God by eating from the Tree of the Knowledge of Good and Evil, He turned the keys of his authority over to Satan, who became the new ruler of this earth.

In order to understand the extent of Satan's authority, let's look at Matthew 4:9[26], which talks about the temptation of our Lord after He had fasted for forty days. Unless Satan actually had the ability to come through on his promises, do you think that our Lord could really have been tempted?

All of these ideas lead to one key point.

This earth is under Satan's control, which explains why we see all kinds of terrible things happening around us.

If God <u>chooses to be bound by the spiritual laws we just discussed</u>, then that provides a clue as to why we need to ask Him for help. We need to ask for help so that He has the <u>legal</u>

---

[26] Matthew 4:9 (NIV) "All this I will give you," he said, "if you will bow down and worship me."

right to step in and do something He is not allowed to do because of the spiritual laws that He chooses to honor.

Now, you might be thinking, "Wait a minute! Didn't you just say that Adam lost the authority to Satan when he sinned, and now you are saying that we suddenly have the authority back again. How can that be?"

The answer lies in the fact that when we accept Jesus as Lord, Galatians 3:13 tells us that "Christ redeemed us from the curse of the law by becoming a curse for us, for it is written: 'Cursed is everyone who is hung on a tree.'"

God immediately gives us a new spirit when we get saved! Even though our body is still on this earth, our spirit is renewed and is governed by the laws of God's kingdom rather than this dying world. **That means that we regain spiritual authority when we accept Jesus, which is why we have the legal right to ask God for help.**

When we ask, we are doing something very important. We are releasing our legal earthly authority to Him so that He can step in and exercise His legal heavenly authority. That is why we must ask.

In order for us to give control of a situation to someone else, a few things must be in place.

- We need to personally be in control, because we cannot give someone else control unless we have it first. Since we were born in this earthly kingdom, our legal dominion is this physical world, meaning we have the legal right to pass our authority to God.

- We need to <u>trust</u> that God has our best interests in mind; we can only do this if we understand His character and believe that He wants the very best for us.

Faith allows us to bridge the gap between the spirit realm and the natural world.

The next chapter explains the biblical basis for faith and how we must approach God on the basis of faith if we are going to get our prayers answered.

Chapter 2d:

Faith and Hope

Faith is trusting God that He has the power to do what he says. Hope is the innate human ability to believe that things are going to get better.

No book on prayer would be complete without discussing the difference between faith and hope.

Understanding that hope is part of this Natural World, whereas faith is part of God's Spiritual Kingdom, explains why God requires us to approach him in faith rather than hope.

Let's give a short overview of each.

Hope

Hope is the innate human ability to believe that things are going to get better. Hope is part of this natural world, and it is a good thing.

Unfortunately, if we look around, it seems that most people place their trust in hope, rather than faith, when in need. They hope that a new job will get them out of debt; they hope that the doctor has the answer; they hope for this, and they hope for that…

God does not want us to stop hoping. After all, Proverbs 13:12[27] says that hope deferred makes the heart sick. Hope is an important part of this human existence, and it is obvious when people have given up hope because it comes though in their conversation, demeanor and actions.

> As believers in Christ, our hope is not in ourselves, our spouse, our job, or anything else. **Our hope is in the ability of God to do what He says. That is the essence of faith.**

Faith

Before we talk about what faith is, let's talk about what faith is not. **Faith is not the denial of reality**. If we receive a bad report from our doctor, simply denying the reality of that report is not faith.

> Faith is the act of trusting God that He will do what He has promised, and that as spirit beings our relationship with Him is by faith.[28]

The idea of faith is fundamental to understanding God's plan of salvation, because this plan could not be carried out without a

---

[27] Proverbs 13:12 (NKJV) "Hope deferred makes the heart sick, but *when* the desire comes, *it is* a tree of life"

[28] Ephesians 2:8-9 (NIV) "For it is by grace you have been saved, through faith— and this is not from yourselves, it is the gift of God— not by works, so that no one can boast."

man who trusted God. Romans 4:3[29] and 4:18-22[30] tell us that Abraham, the father of the Jewish nation, demonstrated his faith by being "fully persuaded that God had power to do what he had promised."

Even though we may not be Jewish by natural birth, Romans 4:16[31] and 4:23-24[32] tell us that if we believe in Jesus, we become part of Abraham's spiritual family and are exercising the "faith of Abraham," for he is spiritually the "father of us all." **As a believer, this is important because the gift of salvation through the Lord Jesus is completely an act of faith.**

As we turn to the New Testament, we see many examples of faith as the Lord and His disciples brought healing to a sick and dying world. A few examples include:

---

[29] Romans 4:3 (NKJV) "For what does the Scripture say? 'Abraham believed God, and it was accounted to him for righteousness.'"

[30] Romans 4:18-22 (NKJV) "Against all hope, Abraham in hope believed and so became the father of many nations, just as it had been said to him, 'So shall your offspring be.' Without weakening in his faith, he faced the fact that his body was as good as dead—since he was about a hundred years old—and that Sarah's womb was also dead. Yet he did not waver through unbelief regarding the promise of God, but was strengthened in his faith and gave glory to God, being fully persuaded that God had power to do what he had promised. This is why 'it was credited to him as righteousness.'"

[31] Romans 4:16 (NIV) "Therefore, the promise comes by faith, so that it may be by grace and may be guaranteed to all Abraham's offspring—not only to those who are of the law but also to those who have the faith of Abraham. He is the father of us all."

[32] Romans 4:23-24 (NIV) " The words 'it was credited to him' were written not for him alone, but also for us, to whom God will credit righteousness—for us who believe in him who raised Jesus our Lord from the dead."

- Mark 5:34 (NKJV) "And He said to her, 'Daughter, <u>your faith has made you well</u>. Go in peace, and be healed of your affliction.'"

- Mark 10:52 (NKJV) "Then Jesus said to him, 'Go your way; <u>your faith has made you well</u>.' And immediately he received his sight and followed Jesus on the road."

- Acts 14:9-10 (NKJV) "This man heard Paul speaking. Paul, observing him intently and seeing that <u>he had faith to be healed</u>, said with a loud voice, 'Stand up straight on your feet!' And he leaped and walked."

As we read these examples, it is clear that people did not receive healing as a result of the faith that Jesus or the disciples had. Rather they received healing as a result of <u>their faith</u>.

We see that when Jesus visited his home town of Nazareth, Matthew 13:58 (NKJV) tells us, "Now He did not do many mighty works there because of their unbelief." This happened because they could not get past the fact that the person who grew up among them was the Savior of the world.

These verses show that our faith will either open or close the door for God to work in our lives.

One other important theme we see throughout the Lord's ministry, as well as the disciples, is the fact that people would be healed after a time of hearing the Word preached. Hearing the Word builds up faith, which opens the door for miracles.

That is why it is important we do two things before we pray for a need. First, we need to dig into God's Word to find out what He thinks about a particular situation; and, second, we need to meditate on what He says in His Word. **By meditating on His Word, we build up our faith so that when we pray, we have faith to believe that God will do what He has promised.**

Examples of Faith vs. Hope

Keep in mind that God expects us to approach Him in faith rather than hope because <u>faith is approaching God on His terms, and hope is approaching God on our terms.</u>

Because we are used to solving the problems of life using the tools of this world, it is only natural that we approach God the same way. The problem is, this does not work.

When we become a believer in Jesus, we have to remind ourselves that the rules of this natural world no longer apply because our spirit has been translated into God's kingdom. That is why we approach Him with an attitude of faith when we have a need in our lives.

Here are a few examples to help demonstrate this point:

1. Sickness:
   a. Hope says: I have cancer, but I hope that the doctors have a treatment for me.
   b. Faith says: Cancer is attacking my body, but by Christ's stripes I have been healed. I know that it is God's will for me to be healthy, and I believe His healing power can heal me through a miracle or through the healing power He works through doctors.

2. Finance:

    a. Hope says: My finances are a mess. I cannot believe I let things get this bad. I hope I can get a better paying job or that someone can help me get out of debt.

    b. Faith says: I am going to start tithing, because I know God promises to rebuke the devourer when I tithe. I have the mind of Christ, and the Holy Spirit lives inside of me. Because of this, I have wisdom, knowledge, and understanding to get out of this mess <u>so that I can be a blessing to others</u>.

3. Marriage:

    a. Hope says: I cannot believe I married this person. We have grown so far apart that I don't even want to try any more. I hope my husband/wife starts doing the right things so that I can start loving them again.

    b. Faith says: God, I am miserable, but I trust that you can help me become the best husband/wife that I can be. Please help me, Holy Spirit, to become the man/woman after your own heart so that I can love, honor, and respect my spouse the way they need me to. (Husbands) Holy Spirit, please help me to love my wife as Christ loved the church and gave himself up for her. (Wives) Holy Spirit, please help me to respect my husband and submit to him, trusting that he will love and respect me according to your Word.

Faith is the recognition that the spiritual always precedes the natural. It is digging into God's Word to find out what He thinks about our situation, and then praying according to His Word. *It is <u>not</u> the denial of reality. <u>It is the recognition that there is a higher plane of existence that believers in Christ Jesus can put their trust in by praying according to God's Word</u>.*

The next chapter explains how to pray in faith according to the Word.

Chapter 2e:

Giving the Word First Place

By aligning our thinking, speaking, and living with the Word of God, we partner with someone who has unlimited power to bring about change in our earthly lives.

If I were asked to provide only one idea about my walk with the Lord, the answer would be "that I have learned to make the Word the ultimate authority in my life."

Hebrews 4:12 (NIV) tells us, "For the word of God is alive and active. Sharper than any double-edged sword, it penetrates even to dividing soul and spirit, joints and marrow; it judges the thoughts and attitudes of the heart." The idea that the Word is alive and has the ability to overcome any earthly problem that stands in opposition to it can take a lifetime to comprehend because every time we think we have it figured out, a new revelation will be around the corner.

By aligning our thinking, speaking, and living with the Word of God, we partner with someone who has unlimited power to bring about change in our earthly lives. Poverty, sickness, depression, and anything else

that is in contradiction to the Word can be overcome by the life-changing power of God.

That's why a time of regular Bible study is crucial to living a victorious Christian life so that, when an attack happens, <u>the Word of God is already residing in us</u>. If we wait until an attack to develop faith in what God says, then we have lost precious time and make overcoming much more difficult. Waiting to develop our faith is like the person who wants a doctor to fix years of bad decisions in a single visit.

The Words of Our Mouth

<u>Our words have the ability to release the power of God into our lives...or to hold us in bondage to the enemies' destructive plan.</u>

Before we can live in victory in this natural world, we must grasp hold of something very important: ***Our words have power.***

Let's examine what God has to say about our words.

1. Mark 11: 22-24 (KJV) "And Jesus answering saith unto them, Have faith in God. For verily I say unto you, That whosoever shall <u>say</u> unto this mountain, Be thou removed, and be thou cast into the sea; and shall not doubt in his heart, but shall believe that those things which he <u>saith</u> shall come to pass; he shall have whatsoever he <u>saith</u>. Therefore I say unto you, what things so ever ye desire, when you pray, believe that ye receive them and ye shall have them."

2. Luke 17:6 (NIV) "If you have faith as small as a mustard seed, you can <u>say</u> to this mulberry tree, 'Be uprooted and planted in the sea' and it will obey you.'"

3. Jeremiah 1:12 (NIV) "The LORD said to me, 'You have seen correctly, for I am watching to see that my Word is fulfilled.'" [The Word of God that believers speak out of their mouths.]

4. 1 John 5:14-15 (NIV) "This is the confidence we have in approaching God: that if we <u>ask</u> anything <u>according to His will</u>, he hears us. And if we know that He hears us—whatever we <u>ask</u>—we know that we have what we <u>asked</u> of Him."

5. John 5:7 (NIV) "If you remain in me and my words remain in you, <u>ask</u> whatever you wish, and it will be done for you."

To reiterate, only when we understand that our words have power to create or destroy will we be able to change our lives. We can speak words that lead to death and destruction, or we can speak words that lead to life and health. Proverbs 18:21[33] makes it very clear that life and death are in the power of the tongue! We must speak God's Words—words of life.

---

[33] Proverbs 18:21 (NKJV) "Death and life *are* in the power of the tongue, And those who love it will eat its fruit."

Chapter 2f:

Hearing God

Learning to hear God is crucial to fulfilling the plan and purpose He has for our lives.

The ability to hear God's voice is something that takes time to develop because it depends on our **belief** that we can actually hear His voice, our **desire** to hear Him, and our **willingness** to be obedient when He speaks.

There are times when I am having a conversation with my wife when she suddenly says, "I don't like your body language," or, "Would you please soften your tone?" If you are a married man, you're probably smiling because you've been told the same thing. Body language and vocal tone say more than words could ever say.

Likewise, when I put my arms around her and allow the full essence of my love to envelop her being, I can tell her I love her without saying a single word.

Just as human communication is a beautifully complex series of interactions, so is our communication with an infinite God.

First Corinthians 6:19 (NIV) asks us, "Do you not know that your bodies are temples of the Holy Spirit, who is in you, whom you have received from God? You are not your own." This means that when we accept Jesus as Lord and Savior, the Holy Spirit comes to live inside of our human bodies. Second Corinthians 1:21-22 (NKJV) also says, " Now He who establishes us with you in Christ and has anointed us is God, who also has sealed us and given us the Spirit in our hearts as a guarantee." It is amazing to think that our prayers do not need to cross time and space to be heard because the one who hears our prayers is living right inside us.

God Primarily Communicates Three Different Ways:

The first is through His **Word**. If you are praying for something that is in complete agreement or contradiction with the Word, then you don't need to hear God speak, because He has already spoken.

It seems that one of the most common ways people choose to ignore God's Word is in the area of relationships. For me, I was faced with a choice after my divorce because I was dating a girl who was not a believer. Even though I prayed for her every day with the hope that she would become a believer, I knew the relationship was wrong because God says not to be unequally yoked together with unbelievers[34] because He knows that two people

---

[34] 2 Corinthians 6:14-16 (NKJV) " Do not be unequally yoked together with unbelievers. For what fellowship has righteousness with lawlessness? And what communion has light with darkness? And what accord has Christ with Belial? Or what part has a believer with an unbeliever? And what agreement has the temple of God with idols? For you are the temple of the living God. As God has said: "I will dwell in them And walk among them. I will be their God, And they shall be My people.""

cannot walk together unless they are in agreement. More importantly, the task of raising kids to love God becomes very difficult if parents are not in agreement. Eventually, I broke off the relationship out of obedience, and God rewarded me with a wonderful godly wife who is my partner as we teach our children to love and know Him.

The second is through the **leading** of the Holy Spirit who lives inside us. His leading became real to me, when after several years of working as an engineer I realized that the career path I was on was not leading where I wanted to go. Psalm 37:23 (KJV) says, "The steps of a good man are ordered by the Lord: and he delighteth in his way." Psalm 37:4 (KJV) says, "Delight thyself also in the Lord: and he shall give thee the desires of thine heart." As I began speaking these verses over my life, I began to have such a strong desire to pursue a particular engineering field that I became consumed with it. This inner desire led to studying on weekends and evenings, resulting in more advanced job opportunities.

There have been other times when I have a desire to study a particular passage of Scripture that helped prepare me for what was to come. Another example was when I had a very difficult problem to solve for work. I struggled with it for several days and finally decided it was time to pray. While praying, I saw the first step in my heart and mind and quickly wrote this down. I returned to praying and saw step after step, each time writing them down until the problem was solved. Why I didn't seek God sooner is beyond me.

These are all examples of the leading of the Holy Spirit.

The third is when the Holy Spirit speaks to us as an **inner voice**. For me, this typically happens when something major is about to occur. On August 19, 2011, I woke out of a sound sleep and heard the words, "I want you to go all in today, Chuck." As an investor, I never go all-in, meaning that I never invest 100% of my cash into the stock market. I attributed this to an overactive imagination and went back to sleep. This happened several more times before I finally woke up for work. All day, I heard the same thing inside my spirit as plainly as someone talking to me. Oddly, I struggled with this because it went against everything I believed, and, frankly, I doubted my ability to hear the Holy Spirit that plainly. Needless to say, I didn't go all-in...resulting in one of the greatest investing mistakes of my career.

A very important way the Holy Spirit speaks is by reminding us of God's Word. A number of years ago, I was on the phone with a friend, and we were talking about going into business together. As soon as I got off the phone I heard the words, "Chuck, I told you not to be unequally yoked together with unbelievers." Consequently, this was the last time I pursued business plans with my friend.

Learning to Hear His Voice

Most importantly, if we feel led to do something that contradicts the Word, then it is not the Holy Spirit speaking to us.

I hope these examples show that there are many ways God chooses to speak to us depending on our personality, desire to listen, and willingness to obey.

One thing I have learned is that hearing God's voice is a learning process. Just as I get some things right and then miss others, so will you. Whenever I miss it, I remind myself that God saw all this before the world began, and I trust Him enough to know that He will not use the really big events of life as a learning experience!

If we are ever going to become all that God intended, it is important that we learn to hear Him. As we understand who we are in Christ, and learn to hear the voice of the Holy Spirit, we develop steadfastness as the trials of life arise.

If you come from a denominational background that taught that miracles and hearing God stopped with the disciples, then I encourage you to read some of the wonderful books on the gifts of the Holy Spirit.

Expect Opposition

When we speak God's Word and trust Him to change our lives, opposition will arise. The spirit world will try to discourage us so that we stop speaking words of faith because they know that victory will never happen if we quit.

John 10:10[35] explains that the forces of darkness come to steal, kill and destroy; meaning that when we begin to speak God's Word in our lives, there is a spirit world standing in opposition to us. Having thousands of years to observe humanity, they

---

[35] John 10:10 (NKJV) "The thief does not come except to steal, and to kill, and to destroy. I have come that they may have life, and that they may have *it* more abundantly."

understand that the best way to defeat a child of God is to get them discouraged.

When we begin to speak God's Word over our lives, expect opposition. **It is not uncommon for things to go from bad to worse when we begin to speak God's Word.** The spirit world knows that if it can get us discouraged, we will give up.

When we dig in our heels and choose to speak the Word, despite the fact that our natural circumstances tell us nothing is getting better, we will achieve spiritual victory. The bigger the need, the bigger the spiritual forces will try to discourage us.

Our words have power, so it is important to not speak the negative thoughts that come to our mind, because the enemy is very good at manipulating feelings. These negative feelings only have power if we choose to speak them.

One of the greatest ways we can keep our faith energized during this time of opposition is by keeping God's promises in front of our eyes and in our ears. A great example of this is when God changed Abram's name to Abraham, which means father of nations. Just as Abraham's faith was rekindled every time he heard his name spoken, our faith will be strengthened when we speak or read God's promises.

The easiest way to put this into practice is to write the Scriptures we are trusting God for on note cards or sticky-notes. By putting these around the house, our faith is built up as we read and speak God's promises.

The more the opposition heats up, the more we need to speak God's Word and not give up hope.

Chapter 2g:

Getting Earthly Help

It does not matter how you receive your answer to prayer, all healing, provision, and wisdom come from God!

A question that often gets asked is the following: _"If I go to the doctor or take medicine, am I still in faith?"_

In order to answer this question, let's ask a couple questions to help drive to the heart of the issue.

1. Who is the source of all healing?

2. Who promises to provide all our needs?

Healing

It's clear from Jesus' ministry that he healed people everywhere He went. As the one who created this earth, it must have broken His heart to see people under the bondage of sickness and disease. Matthew 9:35 (NIV) tells us that "Jesus went through all the towns and villages, teaching in their synagogues, proclaiming the good news of the kingdom and healing every disease and sickness."

Whether healing is received as a supernatural act or it comes through the hand of a doctor or medicine, the <u>power</u> to heal comes from God. The power of certain plants to bring healing was placed into those plants at the time of the creation, just as the wisdom and power of talented doctors and researchers to bring healing comes from God.

Problems arise if we start to put our trust in the doctor or medicine rather than God. <u>As long as we stand unmovable on the fact that the power to heal comes from God, we are in faith.</u>

I had to come to terms with this idea because of shoulder and back injuries I suffered at different times in my life. I listened to healing Scriptures throughout both operations because I knew God was my healer, and I wanted to feed my spirit with the power of His Word.

Before the doctor operated on my shoulder, I was honored to be able to pray with him by thanking God for placing the gifts and talents in him so that he could bring healing to those in need. This prayer encouraged him and yet gave God the glory for my healing.

Because I had the faith to verbalize my trust in God and speak in accordance with His Word, I had incredible success. <u>Healing came from God at the hand of a skilled doctor and medical team!</u>

Provision

Philippians 4:19 (NKJV) tells us, "And my God shall supply all your need according to His riches in glory by Christ Jesus."

James 1:17 (NKJV) says, "Every good gift and every perfect gift is from above, and comes down from the Father of lights, with whom there is no variation or shadow of turning."

These verses explain that <u>God is the source of everything we need,</u> and we can count on Him because He does not change like a shadow that moves throughout the day. Hebrews 13:8 (NKJV) reiterates this fact by telling us, "Jesus Christ *is* the same yesterday, today, and forever."

When we discuss finances, it is important to recognize that <u>God is the source</u> of our financial blessing and our <u>job or business is the channel</u> it comes through. By understanding this, tithing becomes a joy rather than a burden.

If you don't tithe and are suffering one financial setback after another, then it is imperative to start tithing because Malachi 3:8-12[36] explains that God's promises of financial blessing are

---

[36] Malachi 8:3-12 (NKJV) " "Will a man rob God? Yet you have robbed Me! But you say, 'In what way have we robbed You?' In tithes and offerings. You are cursed with a curse, For you have robbed Me, *Even* this whole nation. Bring all the tithes into the storehouse, That there may be food in My house, And try Me now in this," Says the LORD of hosts, "If I will not open for you the windows of heaven And pour out for you *such* blessing That *there will* not *be room* enough *to receive it.* "And I will rebuke the devourer for your sakes, So that he will not destroy the fruit of your ground, Nor shall the vine fail to bear fruit for you in the field," Says the LORD of hosts; [12] "And all nations will call you blessed, For you will be a delightful land," Says the LORD of hosts."

for those who tithe. By not tithing, we open up our finances to the "devourer," meaning that there is a spirit who destroys the finances of those who are not under the covering of God's protection.

We serve a wonderful God who desires to bless us with health and provision as we recognize that He is the source of everything good.

Chapter 2h:

When do We Receive the Answer to Our Prayer?

The spiritual always precedes the natural. We receive the answer by faith **when we pray,** *not when the answer arrives.*

When I am going through a battle, there are moments when I feel a sense of hopelessness because the answer is taking so long to arrive. Very often, these feelings come after times of strong faith as the enemy tries to cast doubt over the situation.

During these times, I try to remind myself when the answer to my prayer actually arrived.

In order to fully understand the idea of when the answer arrives, let's ask two questions:

- Does the answer arrive when we receive the victory? Or...
- Does the answer arrive when we pray?

If we flip back to the chapter on faith, we see that *prayer is reaching into the spiritual world and asking God to change something in the natural so that it lines up with His Word.*

According to Mark 11:24, the answer is received when we pray, not when the answer is received. The NIV says, "Therefore I tell you, whatever you ask for in prayer, <u>believe that you have received</u> it, and it will be yours." The KJV says, "Therefore I say unto you, What things soever ye desire, <u>when ye pray</u>, believe that ye receive *them*, and ye shall have *them*."

<u>Prayer is an act of faith</u> that requires us to lay hold of the answer <u>when we pray</u> long before the answer ever arrives.

What if things don't turn out as you expect?

Life rarely works out like we hope it will. What's more, the Lord told us that in this life *we would have adversity*, but that He would help us overcome.[37]

The Word is clear that we have a spiritual enemy who hates and opposes us because we are created in the image and likeness of God. This enemy will do everything in his power to prevent us from being healthy, prosperous, and passing a love for God on to our children and grandchildren.

Because Adam gave Satan dominion over this natural earthly realm, we are at a distinct disadvantage unless we come to a realization that there is a spiritual battle raging around us all the time. Hope is not lost, however, because the Lord Jesus came to this earth not only to save us from the power of sin, but also to help us live a victorious life. When we get saved, the Lord sends

---

[37] John 16:33 (NIV) "I have told you these things, so that in me you may have peace. In this world you will have trouble. But take heart! I have overcome the world."

the Holy Spirit to live inside our mortal bodies so that we become living, breathing temples of God.

So...what happens when we do everything right and we don't receive the answer to our prayer?

That is the age-old question that so many have struggled with, as they trust God for an answer that never seems to come. It is particularly painful when we see a person of faith die prematurely or we suffer the loss of a child.

At some time in our lives, we all face a major obstacle that brings us to a decision point, and our response will determine the course of events from that moment forward. It is important to remember that **our futures are determined by the choices we make today; and our responses today will determine whether our futures are governed by a faith that is unshakable or whether we live lives of spiritual mediocrity.** As the saying goes, the future is in our hands.

We will have to choose from one of the following two options when that time comes:

- We can choose to explain away our disappointment, or...
- We can dig in our heels and say that God's Word is true no matter what.

Explain Away Disappointment

Most people choose to explain away unanswered prayers because this is easy. By doing this, we are making God fit into our human experience by saying that He doesn't honor His Word all the time, His ways are unknowable, or any other number of platitudes.

We see examples of this throughout history as people of faith dealt with tragedy and turned their backs on the Word by deciding that a life of faith and trusting God did not always work because they didn't get the desired result.

If we take that position, we are saying that the truth of God being the same yesterday, today, and forever is just a nice idea that does not really line up with reality.

Unfortunately, this response sows seeds of mistrust and fear, which will ultimately impact our confidence in God's Word and our ability to trust Him. Whether we realize it or not, people are watching to see how we will respond in a difficult situation. Giving up on God when things don't go our way has far-reaching consequences.

Dig Your Heels In

The correct response to disappointment is to decide that God is faithful and we can trust Him—no matter what happens around us.

Turning back to the beginning of this book, we said that prayer is nothing like our human experience. This means that, no matter what happens in our life, we must trust God's Word regardless what our emotions or experiences are telling us.

Personally, I ran into this when my daughter was struggling with earaches over the course of several months. As a daddy, my heart ached, and I got upset at God because He didn't supernaturally heal my daughter's ears as she was crying in the middle of the night. Emotions are indelibly etched into my heart because of the pain she was experiencing.

The decision point I came to was this... Do I trust God no matter what, or do I say that God is not true to His Word? I stepped back from the situation and asked myself if He had been faithful time and time again in the past, and the answer was a resounding YES!

I chose to stay true to God's Word and trust Him even if my daughter's sobs were telling me something completely different. Once I came to this point, an amazing thing happened. Peace overtook the situation and I began to _rest_ in the truths of His Word, knowing that healing would come either through medicine, the skill of a trained physician, or by a supernatural healing.

That situation impacted my life because it taught me an important lesson that changed the way I look at everything. My daughter ended up getting tubes in her ears, which helped solve the immediate problem, but another hidden problem existed, which was the real source of the sickness. You see, we had a leak in our roof, and the water was dripping on the sheetrock directly above her pillow, causing mold to silently growing day after day. Every night, while my precious daughter lay down to sleep, mold was poisoning her body and causing her to get sick. We ended up fixing the roof, having that moldy section of sheetrock replaced, and she stopped getting sick.

Looking back, I was asking God to supernaturally heal my daughter of a sickness without fixing the very thing that was making her sick. <u>So often we ask God to do something without really examining our lives and asking, "Is there something I need to fix before asking God to perform a miracle?"</u>

After living a life of faith for many years and learning the character and nature of God, the first place I look when I have a problem is at myself—because more often than not, I can fix the problem by changing a few things in my life. How many of our struggles could be solved by reading a Proverb a day to gain wisdom to help with many issues in our lives? There is also a plethora of wonderful books out there to help develop better life skills.

<u>So, for the times when you have done all the right things, exhausted all natural earthly solutions, prayed and asked for God's supernatural intervention, and nothing gets better, then what?</u> **That is the time to dig your heels in, get your speaking in alignment with the Word, ask for wisdom to know if you need to change something in your life and, finally, don't give up!**

In the end, the choice comes down to this: No matter what, will we trust God?

Ephesians 6:13 (NIV) says, "Therefore put on the full (whole) armor of God, so that when the day of evil comes, you may be able to stand your ground, and <u>after you have done everything, to stand.</u>"

Chapter 2i:

Overview

<u>The spiritual always precedes the natural. Prayer is reaching into the spiritual world and asking God to change something in the natural to line up with His Word. Faith is trusting that God has the power to do that which He has promised.</u>

Let's highlight the ideas presented so far:

- God created mankind in His image so that we could fellowship together; a fellowship that was broken when Adam brought sin into the world. Our Heavenly Father sent the Lord Jesus to die for the sin of mankind so that this fellowship could be restored.

- When we receive Jesus as Lord and Savior, our spirit is translated from this earthly kingdom into God's Spiritual Kingdom, allowing Him to send His Holy Spirit to live inside our physical bodies.

- Prayer is the act of talking with God on the basis of righteousness that comes through salvation in Jesus Christ.

- There are two kinds of prayer: relational prayer and need-based prayer. Relational prayer is when we converse with God like we do with a spouse or good friend and is one of the most wonderful parts of being a Christian. Need-based prayer is when we come to God and ask Him to meet our major needs, as well as the needs of daily life.

- Because God created the universe with spiritual and natural laws, He does not step in and help us whenever we have a need. Instead, He waits for us to ask for help. Our request must be in accordance with His Word and must be presented to Him in faith, not hope.

- Once we ask Him for help, it often takes longer for the answer to arrive than we would like because the enemy is actively opposing us, with the hope that we will get discouraged and give up.

- We combat the attacks of doubt and discouragement by meditating on God's promises and thanking Him for the victory, even before it arrives. We can do this because the essence of faith is trusting God to do that which He has promised.

- Proverbs 18:21[38] tells us that our words have the power to bring life or death depending on what we speak, while Isaiah 55:10-11[39] explains that the Word of God is a seed. We know that according to the law of seedtime and

---

[38] Proverbs 18:21 (NKJV) "Death and life *are* in the power of the tongue, And those who love it will eat its fruit."

[39] Isaiah 55:10-11 (NIV) " As the rain and the snow come down from heaven, and do not return to it without watering the earth and making it bud and flourish, so that it yields seed for the sower and bread for the eater, so is my word that goes out from my mouth: It will not return to me empty, but will accomplish what I desire and achieve the purpose for which I sent it."

harvest, which God established in Genesis 8:22,[40] that the words we speak will produce after their kind. If we speak words of discouragement and discontent, then the fruit of these will be more negative feelings.

- It is so important to <u>pray according to God's Word and then to thank and praise God</u> for the answer before it arrives in the natural. By doing this, we are exercising faith according to Hebrews 11:1 (NKJV), which says, "Now faith is the substance of things hoped for, the evidence of things not seen."

Steps to ask God to meet a need:

1. Spend time in God's Word to find out what He says about our situations.

2. Recognize that God is the source of the answer, not anything in the natural. He often works through other people, but the ultimate source of the answer comes from Him.

3. Ask Him for help, which gives Him the ability to work in our lives.

4. Ask in faith by speaking God's Word based upon what we learned in step 1.

5. Continue to speak the Word and thank Him until the answer arrives.

6. Give Him glory once the answer arrives.

---

[40] Genesis 8:22 (NKJV) "While the earth remains, Seedtime and harvest, Cold and heat, Winter and summer, And day and night Shall not cease."

Once we have prayed, we continue to remind God of His promises, but with an attitude of expectancy and thankfulness rather than as a request.

- The first time we pray: "Heavenly Father, According to (insert the Scripture you are standing on) I ask you to (whatever the need)."

- Subsequent times we pray: "Heavenly Father, I thank you that according to (insert the Scripture you are standing on) I have (whatever the need) and I praise you that I have the request that I made of you."

God cares about our needs and loves mankind so much that He sent His own Son to die for the sins of the world. We are reminded of God's love and faithfulness by Romans 8:32 (NKJV), which says, "He who did not spare His own Son, but delivered Him up for us all, how shall He not with Him also freely give us all things?"

Chapter 3:

Word Pictures

Worry, fear, and doubt are the enemies of living a victorious Christian life because they undermine our ability to trust that God will do the very things He promises to do. The following word pictures provide easy ways to visualize the ideas presented in this book. Since God is the source of wisdom, it is important to ask for wisdom whenever we face trials in any part of our lives.

The Hand Prayer

Our hand provides a convenient reminder of what to pray for on a daily basis.

Many years ago, I heard someone explain that God gave us a great reminder of what to pray for on a daily basis...our hand! Like many believers, I had a difficult time knowing what to pray for, and the hand prayer has been a tremendous help.

While the example below is not set in stone, it has worked well for me over the years. Feel free to tailor it to your specific needs and the needs of your family.

Thumb

Because the thumb is the closest finger to the heart, it reminds us to pray for those who are closest to us — our family and close friends.

Index

The index finger is also called the pointer. It reminds us to pray for those who point us to God. This includes our pastors, evangelists, missionaries, etc.

Middle

The middle finger is the tallest finger; in effect it is over all the other fingers. It reminds us to pray for those who are over us in authority. God commands us in 1 Timothy 2:1-3[41] to pray for leaders so that we can live a peaceful life in all godliness and honesty. We pray that our leaders have Godly wisdom and make decisions according to the Word because it is the ultimate authority. We want our leaders to be steadfast, godly people who make wise decisions.

Ring

The ring finger is the weakest of all the fingers. This finger reminds us to pray for the weak by praying for the believers who

---

[41] 1 Timothy 2:1-3 (KJV) "I exhort therefore, that, first of all, supplications, prayers, intercessions, and giving of thanks, be made for all men; For kings, and for all that are in authority; that we may lead a quiet and peaceable life in all godliness and honesty. For this is good and acceptable in the sight of God our Saviour;"

live in persecuted lands, for the nation of Israel that is under constant threat of attack, for those believers in prison, and for the poor, orphans, widows, and the abused. This also reminds us to pray for our military that has been sent to protect those who cannot protect themselves.

Pinky

Finally, we pray for ourselves. **The greatest joy we can have is to fulfill the plan and purpose God has for our lives.** As we go through our day, we should pray for wisdom and sound judgment to make good decisions. We should also ask the Holy Spirit to help us find opportunities to share the Gospel with those in our spheres of influence.

Faith is Like Gardening – Seedtime and Harvest

The process of faith is just like gardening. We prepare the soil of our heart by meditating on the Word of God; plant only the best seeds by speaking God's promises and not words of doubt; water by praising Him for the victory while continuing to speak the Word; and finally reaping a harvest when the victory arrives.

My Dad was an avid gardener, so some of my youngest memories revolve around the garden where my Dad would wear his old boots that were caked with dried mud. Every spring and summer, he diligently prepared the soil, planted seeds, watered, weeded, and finally reaped the harvest we all looked forward to. The law that governs gardening is called "seedtime and harvest."

Genesis 8:22[42] explains that the principle of seedtime and harvest will be in effect as long as we live on planet earth. Equally important, this law governs everything we do in life because the person we are today is the result of choices we made yesterday…seedtime and harvest.

Soil

Year after year, I remember my Dad having loads of compost delivered to the house with the hope that he could turn the clay he started with into beautiful soil.

This is a perfect picture of humanity. It doesn't matter whether a person is a new believer in Christ or has been a Christian for many years but never lived by faith, their "faith soil" is like the clay that my Dad started with.

> If you feel like your faith soil is like clay, don't give up. Like my Dad enriching the soil year after year, each trial-turned-victory is an opportunity to develop your faith. <u>The joy in the process is recognizing that victory always follows a trial…if we don't give up.</u> One day you will wake up and realize that you have the faith of Abraham!

Seed

Becoming a gardener like my Dad, I realized that the quality of the seeds play a major role in the outcome of the harvest. In the days before hybrids, gardeners used a technique called open-pollination to grow the best plants. They would take seeds from

---

[42] Genesis 8:22 (NKJV) "While the earth remains, Seedtime and harvest, Cold and heat, Winter and summer, And day and night Shall not cease."

the best fruit and use them for next year's planting, thus ensuring that only the best seeds got planted year after year.

The same principle applies to the faith realm because the seed we sow is whatever we speak. If we say things like, "I am always sick," or, "I will never get my finances under control," then we will probably get what we are saying. This would be like planting the seeds from sick, diseased plants.

<u>However, if we speak God's Word in our life, then this is like planting seeds from the very best plants.</u>

Isaiah 55:10-13[43] reminds us that His Word is seed He provided for us to sow!

Watering

No gardener would spend the time preparing soil and planting the best seeds only to dump polluted water onto the garden. Yet, that is exactly what happens when we speak words of discouragement and doubt when the answer does not arrive in our expected time frame.

---

[43] Isaiah 55:10-13 (NIV) " As the rain and the snow come down from heaven, and do not return to it without watering the earth and making it bud and flourish, so that it yields seed for the sower and bread for the eater, so is my word that goes out from my mouth: It will not return to me empty, but will accomplish what I desire and achieve the purpose for which I sent it. You will go out in joy and be led forth in peace; the mountains and hills will burst into song before you, and all the trees of the field will clap their hands. Instead of the thornbush will grow the juniper, and instead of briers the myrtle will grow. This will be for the LORD's renown, for an everlasting sign, that will endure forever.""

Just as a loving gardener knows that regular watering with a touch of fertilizer produces the best crop, we need to speak words of life until we see the natural line up with the spiritual.

The best way to water our prayer is to thank and praise God for the answer while continuing to speak His promises before we receive the victory. Just as the gardener waters his plants with the expectation of a harvest, so we should give praise to God with the expectation that His Word will come to pass.

The kingdom of darkness that has dominion in this natural world knows that the best time to get us off track is between the time we pray and the answer arrives. It takes patience and faith to speak God's Word, particularly when we don't see the answer or when things seem to go from bad to worse.

Keeping God's Word in front of us helps keep our faith strong during this waiting time.

Harvest

This is the exciting part. Just as the gardener reaps a harvest after months of trusting the gardening process, we should expect to see the victory if we don't give up because God is faithful.

When the victory arrives, it is important to give God the glory so that others can have their faith strengthened.

David and Goliath

David understood the promises that came as a result of his covenant with God. He also understood the power of his words.

The Power of Words

In 1 Samuel 17, verses 10-11[44] and 16,[45] we are told how Goliath paralyzed the armies of Israel by standing in front of them like a giant bully, hurling insults every morning and evening for forty days. Goliath knew the effect his words had on the armies of Israel.

We see that David also understood the power of his words as he spoke words of faith in response to an enemy that was too large to defeat in the natural.[46]

David also understood that he had a covenant with God that was inherited through Abraham, which meant he had promises of provision and protection, that did not belong to someone outside the covenant. As believers in Christ, Galatians 3:29[47] tells us that we are spiritual descendants of Abraham and heirs of the same covenant; meaning that all the promises God gave to Abraham are ours through Christ Jesus.

---

[44] 1 Samuel 17:10-11 (KJV) " And <u>the Philistine said</u>, I defy the armies of Israel this day; give me a man, that we may fight together. When Saul and all Israel heard those words of the Philistine, <u>they were dismayed, and greatly afraid.</u>

[45] 1 Samuel 17:16 (KJV) "And the Philistine drew near morning and evening, and presented himself forty days."

[46] 1 Samuel 17:45-47 (KJV) " <u>Then said David</u> to the Philistine, Thou comest to me with a sword, and with a spear, and with a shield: but <u>I come to thee in the name of the LORD of hosts, the God of the armies of Israel</u>, whom thou hast defied. <u>This day will the LORD deliver thee into mine hand</u>; and I will smite thee, and take thine head from thee; and I will give the carcases of the host of the Philistines this day unto the fowls of the air, and to the wild beasts of the earth; <u>that all the earth may know that there is a God in Israel</u>. And all this assembly shall know that the LORD saveth not with sword and spear: <u>for the battle is the LORD's</u>, and he will give you into our hands."

[47] Galatians 3:29 (KJV) "And if ye be Christ's, then are ye Abraham's seed, and heirs according to the promise."

We see that David understood the importance of this covenant by calling Goliath an "uncircumcised Philistine"[48] two different times. What David was reminding everyone was that Goliath was outside the covenant and <u>could be defeated because he didn't have the promise of protection that David had</u>.

> Just like David understood that he had special promises from God, we have special promises of God as a result of salvation through the Lord Jesus.

Small Victories Build Your Faith

One of the things David did was to build up the faith and confidence of everyone by recounting the previous times God had delivered him from seemingly impossible circumstances.[49]

---

[48] 1 Samuel 17:26, 36 (KJV) " And David spake to the men that stood by him, saying, What shall be done to the man that killeth this Philistine, and taketh away the reproach from Israel? for who is this <u>uncircumcised</u> Philistine, that he should defy the armies of the living God?" and " Thy servant slew both the lion and the bear: and this <u>uncircumcised</u> Philistine shall be as one of them, seeing he hath defied the armies of the living God."

[49] 1 Samuel 17:32-37 (KJV) " And David said to Saul, Let no man's heart fail because of him; thy servant will go and fight with this Philistine. And Saul said to David, Thou art not able to go against this Philistine to fight with him: for thou art but a youth, and he a man of war from his youth. 34And David said unto Saul, Thy servant kept his father's sheep, and there came a lion, and a bear, and took a lamb out of the flock: And I went out after him, and smote him, and delivered it out of his mouth: and when he arose against me, I caught him by his beard, and smote him, and slew him. Thy servant slew both the lion and the bear: and this uncircumcised Philistine shall be as one of them, seeing he hath defied the armies of the living God. David said moreover, The LORD that delivered me out of the paw of the lion, and out of the paw of the bear, he will deliver me out of the hand of this Philistine. And Saul said unto David, Go, and the LORD be with thee."

Even though his jealous brothers tried to discourage him, we see that this did not deter David from trusting God to help him defeat Goliath.[50]

During smaller tests and trials, it is important for us to do what David did and use these as opportunities to build our faith. These are the best times to learn to hear the voice of the Holy Spirit while developing confidence that God honors His Word.

If we learn to develop faith and hear the voice of the Holy Spirit during smaller trials, we will have confidence like David when he fought Goliath.

The Flaming Arrows of the Enemy

When the enemy shoots a flaming arrow at us, we can either accept it, or use the shield of faith to reject it.

Ephesians 6:16 tells us "In addition to all this, take up the shield of faith, with which you can extinguish all the flaming arrows of the evil one."

So, what does this really mean..... after all, how many of us really have to go into battle where the enemy is shooting arrows at us?

---

[50] 1 Samuel 17:28 (NKJV) "Now Eliab his oldest brother heard when he spoke to the men; and Eliab's anger was aroused against David, and he said, 'Why did you come down here? And with whom have you left those few sheep in the wilderness? I know your pride and the insolence of your heart, for you have come down to see the battle.'"

When a soldier goes into battle, one of the best defensive positions is the high ground with plenty of obstacles to hide behind. It is very difficult to shoot someone who holds this sort of position.

Now, let's look back to WWII at the beaches of Normandy. As the Allies stormed the beaches, they had very few obstacles to hide behind resulting in terrible losses in many cases. In the ultimate act of bravery, we have recorded stories of leaders standing out in the open to draw fire so their men could advance.

As we contrast these two ideas it is clear that the best place to be is behind something safe and the most dangerous position is to be the leader standing out in the open trying to draw fire.

Now, lets apply these ideas to our lives.

The "flaming arrows" that Ephesians talks about include sickness, disease, cancer, poverty, abuse, enslavement, rebellion, theft, and anything else that is contrary to the Word of God.

Whenever one of these flaming arrows comes against us we are faced with a choice:

- Do I accept it (this is the natural, worldly response)

- Do I reject it based upon the Word (this is the spiritual response)

Natural Response

The choice we make is based upon what comes out of our mouths and the attitude of our heart since "...out of the abundance of the heart his mouth speaks." (Luke 6:45 NKJV)

How often do you hear people say, "I caught a cold," "my cancer," "I will always be broke," or, "I will never get out of this situation."

When we say these things, we are using the power of our words to stand defenseless in front of a flaming arrow with the result that it <u>will</u> hit us..... because <u>we</u> said it would!

Spiritual Response

When the enemy sends flaming arrows our direction, we need to stop saying we "caught this" or "caught that" and use the shield of faith to reject these arrows so they have no ability to harm us.

Instead, we reject these arrows by speaking the Word against them, thereby placing the shield of faith between the arrow and us. This is very much like a soldier having the strong defensible position we talked about earlier.

What's more, the Word says that the shield of faith will *extinguish* these flaming arrows! This means that when spiritual attacks come, the shield of faith not only protects us but it causes these attacks to reduce and reduce until they eventually stop just like a fire will eventually go out if we keep spraying water on it.

By using the power of our words, we can overcome the attacks of this life by speaking the Word in faith and not giving up (see Section 2e – Giving the Word First Place).

A Lifelong Dream

Two weeks after finishing the manuscript for this book, God opened the door to run for public office as a State Representative in Oklahoma. The idea of public service had been something God placed in the heart of my wife and I many, many years ago.

As we began looking at all the various aspects of the campaign, it became obvious that we were totally unprepared for the battle that lay ahead because of the overall immensity of this project, but also because of the financial requirements. The Holy Spirit spoke to our hearts and told us that our support for this campaign would come from totally unexpected places, and the outcome was in His hands. Our job was to pray and stand for righteousness.

The weight of this campaign was more than anything we had ever experienced, and we made the decision to take the first part of the week and dedicate it to prayer. Every Monday before we started campaigning, we would take time to intercede for the campaign, our volunteers, the people we would meet, and finally for the campaign finances.

We also would hold hands and pray every day before campaigning through neighborhoods.

The results were truly amazing, as we saw one miraculous event after another. What impressed me the most was when we didn't take time out of our day to pray on Monday or when we didn't pray before campaigning through neighborhoods. On those days it felt like we were walking through molasses as people would not be receptive to our message. Realizing what was going on, we would stop and pray—and the situation would change almost immediately.

---

[51] Ephesians 6:16 (NIV) says "In addition to all this, take up the shield of faith, with which you can extinguish all the flaming arrows of the evil one."

This whole experience took our faith and prayer life to a whole new level as we saw God's hand of faithfulness in a very tangible way. He gave us victory in an election that very few believed we could win.

> On election night, I did not watch the election results come in because my wife and I had done that which we were called to do. ***We knew that no matter the outcome, we already won because we had been obedient.***

A Cry for Help

I want to share a wonderful example of God's deliverance a split second before disaster.

Back in 1989, I fell asleep while driving home on a rainy day in Indiana around 7:00 a.m., going roughly sixty-five miles per hour. When I awoke, my car was speeding through waist high grass on the side of the highway, and my immediate reaction was to steer the car back onto the highway. I quickly realized that I was sliding in mud and had no control. Even though it was almost thirty years ago, I can still run through the experience in my mind like it was yesterday. What really scared me was the fact that the car was on a trajectory heading right for the concrete embankment of an overpass.

As I was rapidly going up the embankment I remember thinking, "I'm going to run right into the overpass." Without thinking, I shouted out, "Lord, please cover me with the blood." I cannot give an earthly explanation as to what happened next, but the car stopped almost instantly, and I never struck the overpass. The car slid down the embankment into a large concrete drainage ditch, and I was able to call a wrecker who pulled the car out. To this day, I still marvel at God's goodness to protect me.

I share this story because my response was not rehearsed, and I certainly did not have time to find a book on prayer. What was inside me came out of my mouth. That is why we need to fill our hearts and minds with God's Word and teaching during easy times. Tough times will come, and whatever is inside of us will come out!

Chapter 4:

Prayer Examples

Pray these Prayers Over Your Children

Heavenly Father, I come to you in Jesus' name. I thank you for my children and the plan you have for their lives (Jeremiah 29:11).

I pray for (insert names of children) and commit them to you. By faith, I also pray for my grandchildren and great grandchildren (Jeremiah 1:5). Thank you that they all will love, honor, and serve you all the days of their lives (Luke 10:27). I thank you that your Word, which is spoken into their lives will not return void (Isaiah 55:11). I thank you that they only marry godly spouses because your Word says to not be unequally yoked together with a nonbeliever (2 Corinthians 6:14). I thank you they fulfill your commandment to train their children in the nurture and admonition of the Lord and, as my future generations are trained in the ways of God, they all come to know you as their personal Lord and Savior (Proverbs 22:6).

I thank you they will become (insert occupations) and that you will use them to change their worlds for the Gospel of Christ (Mark 16:15). I thank you their steps are ordered of you (Psalm

37:23), and the plans you have for them are to prosper them and give them a hope and a future (Jeremiah 29:11). I thank you for the gifts and talents you've placed in them and ask that they will use these talents for your glory as they fulfill the plan and purpose you've created them for (Proverbs 18:16).

I thank you that (names) delights in you and that you fulfill the desires of their heart as they walk with you (Psalm 37:4). I also thank you that they do not walk in the counsel of the ungodly, nor stand in the way of sinners, nor sit in the seat of the scornful. Rather, their delight is in your Word, which they study every day (Psalm 1).

I pray you will rid and deliver (insert names) from the hand of strange children and that ungodly people do not have an influence in their lives (Psalm 144:11-12).

I thank you that no weapon formed against them will prosper (Isaiah 54:17) and they will enjoy supernatural health, and joy (Romans 15:13) so others will want to know you because they see the power of God working in their lives (Matthew 5:16). I thank you that they honor their parents knowing that you promise them long lives if they do this (Ephesians 6:2-3).

Deuteronomy 28:32 tells us the curse of the law, which comes on people for rejecting God, is that their children are taken from them. I thank you that, as a believer in Christ, Jesus has redeemed my family from the curse of the law, which means that my children will never be taken from me in either a spiritual or physical sense (Galatians 3:13).

I thank you for giving me wisdom as I train my children and future generations (James 1:5) and that as they are trained in the Word of God, they have great peace (Isaiah 54:13).

In Jesus' name, amen.

Pray These for Yourself and Your Family Members

Heavenly Father, I come to you in Jesus name and thank you for my family.

By faith, I cover (insert names of family members) with the precious blood of Jesus. I bring to bear the power of the blood of the Lord Jesus (Ephesians 2:13, Hebrews 9:11-28, Revelation 5:9, Revelation 12:11) against principalities, powers, rulers of darkness, and spiritual wickedness in the high places (Ephesians 6:12). I bind and rebuke anyone or anything, spiritual or natural, that would try to cause any operation contrary to the Word of God in my life or the lives of my family. I bind and rebuke these forces because the Word says that what is bound on earth will be bound in heaven and what is loosed on earth will be loosed in heaven (Matthew 18:18).

God, I thank you for my job, and the opportunity I have to provide for my family (or, I thank you for the job you've given me as I take care of my home and the opportunity to raise my children) (1 Timothy 5:8). Please help me to be diligent and wise as I provide for my family (Proverbs 28:19). I also ask you to help me to bring the joy of the Lord into my home (Colossians 3:16). Help me to be a great parent and to not bring frustration to my family. (Husbands: may I love my wife the way she needs me to love her / Wives: help me to submit to my husband and show him respect) (Colossians 3:17-21). I pray for wisdom throughout the day so that I can find creative solutions to the problems that arise (James 1:5).

The fruit of the Spirit is love, joy, peace, patience, kindness, goodness, faithfulness, and self-control (Galatians 5:22). I pray that the fruit of the Spirit dwells in and flows through me as I interact with people throughout the day, but especially my family (Ephesians 1:17-18).

As an ambassador of Christ, I know that I am a light in a dark world. I ask that you would help me train my family to understand that they also are ambassadors for Christ (Matthew 5:13-16).

I thank you that you will complete the good work you started in the lives of (insert names) (Philippians 1:6). I know that our home is in heaven, and I pray that every member of my family will keep you on their hearts and minds throughout the day, because we know that this leads to life and peace (Romans 8:6).

I know you told us that suffering and persecution will happen. I thank you that the sufferings of this life are nothing, when compared with the glory that will be revealed in us (Romans 8:18).

Father, I thank you again for my family, and I am excited for the plan you have for our lives because we can trust you knowing that a man's heart devises his ways, but the Lord orders his steps (Proverbs 16:9)

In Jesus' name, amen.

Pray These Scriptures for Healing

MARK 16:17-18 explains that "these signs shall follow them that believe…they will lay their hands on the sick, and they will recover." A point of contact is important when praying for someone so that the power of God can flow through you and into the person with the need. If the person needing healing is yourself, then lay a hand on the area needing healing.

Heavenly Father, I come to you in Jesus' name.

Faith means that I trust that you have the power to do what you have promised.

I thank you that you care about me and I have faith in your Word, which promises that it is your will for me to be healed and to live a healthy life. While you were on this earth, Scripture tells us many times that you healed all who came to you in need of healing (Matthew 4:23-24, Matthew 13:58, Mark 5:34, Mark 6:6, Mark 10:52, Luke 6:19, Luke 8:25, Acts 5:16, and Acts 14:9).

Because I have made the LORD my dwelling place and the Most High my refuge, I thank you that with long life you satisfy me and show me your salvation (Psalm 91:9-16).

Your Word also tells us that healing is the "children's bread' (Matthew 15:26). Since bread is the staple of life, we know that healing is something that should be part of our daily lives.

I thank you for giving us your Word so we can understand that healing is your will for our lives. I pray for wisdom to know if there is anything I need to change in terms of diet or lifestyle so I can live a healthy life (James 1:5).

The Word of God says when I pray according to God's will that you hear me, and if you hear me, I have the healing that I am requesting of you (1 John 5:14-15). Your Word also says that the works that you did, we shall do, and if we ask anything in your name you will do it (John 14:12-14). Therefore, I ask in Jesus' name for a complete and total healing and restoration for my body.

The Word also says my body is a temple of the Holy Spirit and it has been bought with a price (1 Corinthians 6:19-20). There-fore, sickness and disease have no dominion over this body.

Romans 8:11 says the God who raised Christ Jesus from the dead will quicken my mortal body through His Spirit who dwells in me. The word "quicken" means to give life, to cause to live, and to make alive. I lay hold on this promise by faith and command my body to live, to be made alive, and be strong.

Lord Jesus, I thank you that by your stripes I have been healed (1 Peter 2:24) and that your plans are to give me a hope and a future (Jeremiah 29:11).

Your Word says if I say to the mountain of sickness to be removed and thrown into the sea, and if I don't doubt in my heart, I will have what I ask for because I pray in accordance with your will (Mark 11:23). Therefore, I say to sickness and disease: You have no part in this body. I bind and rebuke (insert sickness) and forbid it to live or have any effect on this body. I say, body, you are the temple of the Holy Spirit. Be healed, healthy, and restored in Jesus' name.

Heavenly Father, I stand in agreement with your Word, and I accept your healing into my body. Please continue to give me wisdom to speak only words of faith, and to make any lifestyle changes necessary to support this healing.

I praise you for healing me and thank you for your Son, the Lord Jesus. For it is by His stripes that I have been healed (Isaiah 53:5).

In Jesus' name, Amen.

Pray these Scriptures Over Our Nation

(Special Thanks to Senator Nathan Dahm for Helping Write this Prayer)

Heavenly Father, I come to You in Jesus' name

Salvation & Offices

Your Word tells us to pray for all men, for kings and all who are in authority so that we can lead peaceful lives in all Godliness and Holiness (1 Tim 2:1). Because it is Your will that none should perish but that all would come to the knowledge of truth (1 Tim 2:4), I pray that you would send laborers across the paths of our leaders (Luke 10:2). I pray for the President and Vice-President, the Cabinet members, members of Congress and staff, the Supreme Court justices and other federal judges; as well as for our State and local officials: the Governor and Executive branch members, members of our State Legislature, our State judges, Mayors and County officers. I pray that our School Board members, administrators and teachers would have boldness to proclaim your truths because they have such influence over our young people.

Ungodly Leaders

I pray that those laborers would boldly proclaim the Gospel of Jesus Christ (Eph 6:19), for it is the power of God unto salvation for all that would believe (Rom 1:16). I ask Heavenly Father (Phil 4:6) that You would raise up new leaders with a heart for God who will lead according to your Word (Acts 13:22). And for those who will not fulfill Your will, who make unjust laws, who oppress the poor, who operate in corruption and who violate their oath, I ask that hidden things would be revealed (Matt 10:26, Mark 4:22, Luke 8:17, Isaiah 2:1-2) so that they can see the light of the Gospel of the Glory of God (2 Cor 4:1-6). I pray that our leaders would not make unjust laws or oppress the poor because we know that judgement will come as a result of this.

Godly Leaders

For those leaders who are following Your will and plan, I ask for divine protection over their lives and that You will deliver them from every evil work that we <u>know</u> will come against them (2 Tim 4:18). I pray that no weapon formed against them shall prosper (Is 54:15) and every tongue that rises against them shall be shown to be in the wrong (Is 54:17). I pray that they will abide in the secret place of the Most High under the shadow of the Almighty and that a thousand may fall at their side and ten thousand at their right hand but it shall not come near them (Ps 91:1,7,12).

Wisdom

I pray that our leaders would be granted the spirit of wisdom and revelation in the knowledge of You and that the eyes of their understanding would be enlightened to know the hope of Your calling (Eph 1:17-18). That those who are lacking wisdom would receive Godly wisdom as they ask it of You who gives wisdom freely to all who ask (James 1:5). I rejoice for the righteous leaders we currently have (Prov 29:2) never ceasing to give thanks for their faith in the Lord Jesus Christ and their love to all who believe.

Nation

I thank You that as those of us who call ourselves by your name humble ourselves and pray, seek Your face and turn from our wicked ways, that You will forgive our sins and heal our land (2 Chron 7:14).

I thank you and ask for all these things in Jesus' Name, Amen

Chapter 5:

Creating Your Own Prayer

Creating your own prayer is straightforward if you follow these general guidelines. Of course, tweak this to meet your own special requirements.

Preparation Work

Before you write out your prayer, dig into the Word and find specific promises related to your need.

Read the verses before and after the promises you are standing on to make sure you are not taking these promises out of context. If a verse is read by itself rather than as part of the chapter, it is easy to apply this promise to something that it was never intended for. By reading the verses before and after a verse, this error can be avoided.

Build Your Prayer

Step 1.   Greet God just like you would another person.

a. While greeting God, it is important to say that we come to Him "in Jesus' name" because our basis to approach Him is not because of our own righteousness, but because of the righteousness that comes from being a believer in Christ.

Step 2. Honor Him by explaining that you recognize that He has the power to meet your need.

    a. Acknowledging that God is the source of meeting your need is crucial to receiving the answer.

    b. Thanking Him for the opportunity to bring your need to Him in prayer is another form of honor.

Step 3. Explain your need to Him and ask Him for help.

    a. This is where we explain our need to Him. Don't spend a lot of time on this step because He already knows what we have need of.

    b. By asking Him for help, we are releasing our earthly authority to Him. This allows Him to step in and help.

Step 4. Create a separate paragraph for each promise you find that applies to your need.

    a. This is where we remind God of what He said about our situation.

    b. When we pray, we are asking God to step in and help. Because He watches over His Word to perform it, He loves when we take time to remind Him of His Word.

c.   Because our words have power, we are using this spiritual law to speak God's Word into our situation.

Step 5.   Thank Him for the promises in His Word and for the answer He is going to provide.

a.   Every prayer should begin and end by thanking God. After we remind God of His Word, it is very important that we tell Him " thank you."

Using the prayer examples above and these steps, you will be able to develop a prayer to meet any need you may have. God's Word has power, and we can live victorious lives by applying it to our lives!

Appendix A:

How to Accept Jesus as Lord

In the Beginning - God's Perfect Plan

God's plan was to have an intimate face-to-face relationship with mankind, which is how things were before Adam and Eve sinned. Genesis 1:26 tells us, " Then God said, 'Let us make mankind in our image, in our likeness.'" I believe the reason God created man in His image and likeness was so that He could have a relationship with beings that could choose to have a relationship with Him.

After God made mankind but before Adam fell, they enjoyed such an intimate relationship that they would walk in the cool of the day[52] just like friends might sit around a table enjoying a cup of coffee.

---

[52] Genesis 3:8 (KJV) " [8]And they heard the voice of the LORD God walking in the garden in the cool of the day: and Adam and his wife hid themselves from the presence of the LORD God amongst the trees of the garden."

Sin and Separation from God

After the fall of mankind, everything changed. Adam was banished from Eden and his face-to-face walks with God came to an abrupt end. The intimate relationship mankind had with our creator was gone and the curse of sin and death came on the earth.

When man sinned, a division was created between God and mankind that cannot be crossed except by accepting Jesus Christ as Lord and Savior.

Romans 3:23 (KJV) tell us "For all have sinned, and come short of the glory of God."

Romans 3:10 (KJV) says "As it is written, There is none righteous, no, not one."

Romans 6:23 (NIV) "For the wages of sin is death, but the gift of God is eternal life in Christ Jesus our Lord." These verses tell us that no one is exempt from the destructive effects of sin.

Finally, 1 John 1: 8-9 (NIV) reiterates this fact by telling us "If we claim to be without sin, we deceive ourselves and the truth is not in us. If we confess our sins, he is faithful and just and will forgive us our sins and purify us from all unrighteousness."

God's Free Gift of Salvation

When pondering what happened during these early days, we need to keep coming back to one crucial fact. I believe that the fall of mankind created a tremendous emptiness in the heart of God and He yearns to have that intimate relationship with mankind restored. Man's fall also created a huge void in the heart of every person. A void that can only be filled with a personal relationship with Jesus Christ, but which people try to fill with work, activities, and life's various pursuits.

Because of God's desire to restore His relationship with mankind, He sent His only Son to die a sacrificial death for the sins of all mankind. This sacrifice bridged the division that existed between God and man. <u>The only requirement placed on each individual is whether to choose or reject this free gift of salvation.</u>

John 3:16-18 (NIV) says " For God so loved the world that he gave his one and only Son, that whoever believes in him shall not perish but have eternal life. For God did not send his Son into the world to condemn the world, but to save the world through him. Whoever believes in him is not condemned, but whoever does not believe stands condemned already because they have not believed in the name of God's one and only Son."

Second Peter 3:9 (NIV) states, "The Lord is not slow in keeping his promise, as some understand slowness. He is patient with you, not wanting anyone to perish, but everyone to come to repentance." <u>Clearly it is God's desire for everyone to accept Jesus and have their sins forgiven.</u>

First Timothy 2:5 (KJV) says, "For there is one God, and one mediator between God and men, the man Christ Jesus," and John 14:6 (NIV) tells us, "Jesus answered, 'I am the way and the truth and the life. No one comes to the Father except through me.'" John 3:36 (NIV) clearly states, "Whoever believes in the Son has eternal life, but whoever rejects the Son will not see life, for God's wrath remains on them." Mark 16:16 (NIV) says, "Whoever believes and is baptized will be saved, but whoever does not believe will be condemned." These verses make it very clear that the choice is up to each person.

Finally, Romans 10:9-10 (NASB) says "that if you confess with your mouth Jesus as Lord, and believe in your heart that God raised Him from the dead, you will be saved; for with the heart a person believes, resulting in righteousness, and with the mouth he confesses, resulting in salvation."

How to accept Jesus as Lord and Savior:

1. Admit you are a sinner and need your sins forgiven.

2. Believe that Jesus Christ died on the Cross and rose from the grave.

3. Acknowledge that Jesus Christ is the only way to God, and commit the rest of your life to Him.

Living a Life in Christ

A life committed to living for God is wonderful, yet will be full of trials that can be overcome through prayer and God's Word.

The New Testament compares it to competing in a sports event. Hebrews 12:1-2 (NIV) tells us, "Therefore, since we are surrounded by such a great cloud of witnesses, let us throw off everything that hinders and the sin that so easily entangles. And let us run with perseverance the race marked out for us, fixing our eyes on Jesus, the pioneer and perfecter of faith. For the joy set before him he endured the cross, scorning its shame, and sat down at the right hand of the throne of God."

What a great adventure to live for the Lord Jesus!

Appendix B:

Scriptures from the Word of God

Building Your Faith

Proverbs 3:1-6

My son, do not forget my teaching, but keep my commands in your heart, for they will prolong your life many years and bring you prosperity. Let love and faithfulness never leave you; bind them around your neck, write them on the tablet of your heart. Then you will win favor and a good name in the sight of God and man. Trust in the LORD with all your heart and lean not on your own understanding; in all your ways acknowledge him, and he will make your paths straight.

Deuteronomy 6:5-9

Love the LORD your God with all your heart and with all your soul and with all your strength. These commandments that I give you today are to be upon your hearts. Impress them on your children. Talk about them when you sit at home and when you walk along the road, when you lie down and when you get up. Tie them as symbols on your hands and bind them on your foreheads. Write them on the doorframes of your houses and on your gates.

Isaiah 55:10-11

As the rain and the snow come down from heaven, and do not return to it without watering the earth and making it bud and flourish, so that it yields seed for the sower and bread for the eater, so is my word that goes out from my mouth: It will not return to me empty, but will accomplish what I desire and achieve the purpose for which I sent it.

Psalm 19:14

May the words of my mouth and the meditation of my heart be pleasing in your sight, O Lord, my Rock and my Redeemer.

Hebrews 4:12

For the word of God is living and active. Sharper than any double-edged sword, it penetrates even to dividing soul and spirit, joints and marrow; it judges the thoughts and attitudes of the heart.

Psalm 119:97-98

Oh, how I love your law! I meditate on it all day long. Your commands make me wiser than my enemies, for they are ever with me.

James 1:25

But the man who looks intently into the perfect law that gives freedom, and continues to do this, not forgetting what he has heard, but doing it—he will be blessed in what he does.

Psalm 119:171-172

May my lips overflow with praise, for you teach me your decrees. May my tongue sing of your word, for all your commands are righteous.

Jeremiah 23:28

Let the prophet who has a dream tell his dream, but let the one who has my word speak it faithfully. For what has straw to do with grain?" declares the LORD.

Matthew 8:8

The centurion replied, "Lord, I do not deserve to have you come under my roof. But just say the word, and my servant will be healed.

Romans 10:17

Consequently, faith comes from hearing the message, and the message is heard through the word of Christ.

Luke 17:6

He replied, "If you have faith as small as a mustard seed, you can say to this mulberry tree, "Be uprooted and planted in the sea,' and it will obey you.

Mark 11:22-24

"Have faith in God," Jesus answered. "I tell you the truth, if anyone says to this mountain, 'Go, throw yourself into the sea,' and does not doubt in his heart but believes that what he says will happen, it will be done for him. Therefore I tell you, whatever you ask for in prayer, believe that you have received it, and it will be yours.

Jeremiah 1:12

The LORD said to me, "You have seen correctly, for I am watching to see that my word is fulfilled."

Isaiah 43:26

Review the past for me, let us argue the matter together; state the case for your innocence.

Freedom From Fear

Isaiah 41:10

So do not fear, for I am with you; do not be dismayed, for I am your God. I will strengthen you and help you; I will uphold you with my righteous right hand.

Isaiah 43:1-3

But now, this is what the LORD says- he who created you, O Jacob, he who formed you, O Israel: "Fear not, for I have redeemed you; I have summoned you by name; you are mine. When you pass through the waters, I will be with you; and when you pass through the rivers, they will not sweep over you. When you walk through the fire, you will not be burned; the flames will not set you ablaze. For I am the LORD, your God, the Holy One of Israel, your Savior; I give Egypt for your ransom, Cush and Seba in your stead.

Isaiah 41:13

For I am the LORD, your God, who takes hold of your right hand and says to you, Do not fear; I will help you.

Psalm 23:4

Even though I walk through the valley of the shadow of death, I will fear no evil, for you are with me; your rod and your staff, they comfort me.

Matthew 10:29-31

Are not two sparrows sold for a penny? Yet not one of them will fall to the ground apart from the will of your Father. And even the very hairs of your head are all numbered. So don't be afraid; you are worth more than many sparrows.

Romans 8:15

For you did not receive a spirit that makes you a slave again to fear, but you received the Spirit of sonship. And by him we cry, "Abba, Father."

John 14:27

Peace I leave with you; my peace I give you. I do not give to you as the world gives. Do not let your hearts be troubled and do not be afraid.

Isaiah 54:14

In righteousness you will be established: Tyranny will be far from you; you will have nothing to fear. Terror will be far removed; it will not come near you.

Isaiah 54:17

No weapon forged against you will prevail, and you will refute every tongue that accuses you. This is the heritage of the servants of the LORD, and this is their vindication from me, declares the LORD.

God's Goodness

Matthew 10:29-31

Are not two sparrows sold for a penny? Yet not one of them will fall to the ground apart from the will of your Father. And even the very hairs of your head are all numbered. So don't be afraid; you are worth more than many sparrows.

Isaiah 61:3

And provide for those who grieve in Zion- to bestow on them a crown of beauty instead of ashes, the oil of gladness instead of mourning, and a garment of praise instead of a spirit of despair. They will be called oaks of righteousness, a planting of the LORD for the display of his splendor.

Romans 8:1-2

Therefore, there is now no condemnation for those who are in Christ Jesus, because through Christ Jesus the law of the Spirit of life set me free from the law of sin and death.

Philippians 1:6

Being confident of this, that he who began a good work in you will carry it on to completion until the day of Christ Jesus.

Ephesians 2:4-7

But because of his great love for us, God, who is rich in mercy, made us alive with Christ even when we were dead in transgressions—it is by grace you have been saved. And God raised us up with Christ and seated us with him in the heavenly realms in Christ Jesus, in order that in the coming ages he might show the incomparable riches of his grace, expressed in his kindness to us in Christ Jesus.

Psalm 31:19

How great is your goodness, which you have stored up for those who fear you, which you bestow in the sight of men on those who take refuge in you.

Romans 8:32

He who did not spare his own Son, but gave him up for us all—how will he not also, along with him, graciously give us all things?

Lamentations 3:22-25

Because of the LORD's great love we are not consumed, for his compassions never fail. They are new every morning; great is your faithfulness. I say to myself, "The LORD is my portion; therefore I will wait for him." The LORD is good to those whose hope is in him, to the one who seeks him.

Isaiah 40:29-31

He gives strength to the weary and increases the power of the weak. Even youths grow tired and weary, and young men stumble and fall; but those who hope in the LORD will renew their strength. They will soar on wings like eagles; they will run and not grow weary, they will walk and not be faint.

Matthew 11:28-30

"Come to me, all you who are weary and burdened, and I will give you rest. Take my yoke upon you and learn from me, for I am gentle and humble in heart, and you will find rest for your souls. For my yoke is easy and my burden is light."

Romans 8:37-39

No, in all these things we are more than conquerors through him who loved us. For I am convinced that neither death nor life, neither angels nor demons, neither the present nor the future, nor any powers, neither height nor depth, nor anything else in all creation, will be able to separate us from the love of God that is in Christ Jesus our Lord.

Romans 5:8

But God demonstrates his own love for us in this: While we were still sinners, Christ died for us.

James 1:17

Every good and perfect gift is from above, coming down from the Father of the heavenly lights, who does not change like shifting shadows.

Romans 8:28

And we know that in all things God works for the good of those who love him, who have been called according to his purpose.

John 3:16-17

"For God so loved the world that he gave his one and only Son, that whoever believes in him shall not perish but have eternal life. For God did not send his Son into the world to condemn the world, but to save the world through him.

Psalm 23:1-3

The LORD is my shepherd, I shall not be in want. He makes me lie down in green pastures, he leads me beside quiet waters, he restores my soul. He guides me in paths of righteousness for his name's sake.

John 14:2-3

In my Father's house are many rooms; if it were not so, I would have told you. I am going there to prepare a place for you. And if I go and prepare a place for you, I will come back and take you to be with me that you also may be where I am.

1 Corinthians 2:9

However, as it is written: "No eye has seen, no ear has heard, no mind has conceived what God has prepared for those who love him"

2 Corinthians 1:20

For no matter how many promises God has made, they are "Yes" in Christ. And so through him the "Amen" is spoken by us to the glory of God.

2 Corinthians 5:17

Therefore, if anyone is in Christ, he is a new creation; the old has gone, the new has come!

Jeremiah 1:12

The LORD said to me, "You have seen correctly, for I am watching to see that my word is fulfilled."

Isaiah 54:14

In righteousness you will be established: Tyranny will be far from you; you will have nothing to fear. Terror will be far removed; it will not come near you.

Healing

Matthew 15:29-31

Jesus left there and went along the Sea of Galilee. Then he went up on a mountainside and sat down. Great crowds came to him, bringing the lame, the blind, the crippled, the mute and many others, and laid them at his feet; and he healed them. The people were amazed when they saw the mute speaking, the crippled made well, the lame walking and the blind seeing. And they praised the God of Israel.

Romans 8:11 (KJV)

But if the Spirit of him that raised up Jesus from the dead dwell in you, he that raised up Christ from the dead shall also quicken **(Strongs defines quicken as: to revitalize, make alive, give life)** your mortal bodies by his Spirit that dwelleth in you.

Galatians 3:13

Christ redeemed us from the curse of the law by becoming a curse for us, for it is written: "Cursed is everyone who is hung on a tree."

3 John 1:2

Dear friend, I pray that you may enjoy good health and that all may go well with you, even as your soul is getting along well.

1 John 4:4

You, dear children, are from God and have overcome them, because the one who is in you is greater than the one who is in the world.

Isaiah 61:3

And provide for those who grieve in Zion- to bestow on them a crown of beauty instead of ashes, the oil of gladness instead of mourning, and a garment of praise instead of a spirit of despair. They will be called oaks of righteousness, a planting of the LORD for the display of his splendor.

John 14:12-14

I tell you the truth, anyone who has faith in me will do what I have been doing. He will do even greater things than these, because I am going to the Father. And I will do whatever you ask in my name, so that the Son may bring glory to the Father. You may ask me for anything in my name, and I will do it.

Isaiah 53:4-5

Surely he took up our infirmities and carried our sorrows, yet we considered him stricken by God, smitten by him, and afflicted. But he was pierced for our transgressions, he was crushed for our iniquities; the punishment that brought us peace was upon him, and by his wounds we are healed.

Luke 6:19

And the people all tried to touch him, because power was coming from him and healing them all.

Matthew 10:1

He called his twelve disciples to him and gave them authority to drive out evil spirits and to heal every disease and sickness.

Mark 16:17-18

And these signs will accompany those who believe: In my name they will drive out demons; they will speak in new tongues; they will pick up snakes with their hands; and when they drink deadly poison, it will not hurt them at all; they will place their hands on sick people, and they will get well.

Matthew 8:17

This was to fulfill what was spoken through the prophet Isaiah: "He took up our infirmities and carried our diseases."

Matthew 21:21-22

Jesus replied, "I tell you the truth, if you have faith and do not doubt, not only can you do what was done to the fig tree, but also you can say to this mountain, 'Go, throw yourself into the sea,' and it will be done. If you believe, you will receive whatever you ask for in prayer."

Mark 9:23

"'If you can?' said Jesus. 'Everything is possible for him who believes.'"

Matthew 17:20-21

He replied, "Because you have so little faith. I tell you the truth, if you have faith as small as a mustard seed, you can say to this mountain, 'Move from here to there' and it will move. Nothing will be impossible for you."

Mark 11: 22-23

"Have faith in God," Jesus answered. "I tell you the truth, if anyone says to this mountain, 'Go, throw yourself into the sea,' and does not doubt in his heart but believes that what he says will happen, it will be done for him."

Philippians 4:6-7

Do not be anxious about anything, but in everything, by prayer and petition, with thanksgiving, present your requests to God. And the peace of God, which transcends all understanding, will guard your hearts and your minds in Christ Jesus.

Mark 11:24

Therefore I tell you, whatever you ask for in prayer, believe that you have received it, and it will be yours.

John 8:36

So if the Son sets you free, you will be free indeed.

Romans 8:1

Therefore, there is now no condemnation for those who are in Christ Jesus.

Mark 16:20

Then the disciples went out and preached everywhere, and the Lord worked with them and confirmed his word by the signs that accompanied it.

Isaiah 54:17

No weapon forged against you will prevail, and you will refute every tongue that accuses you. This is the heritage of the servants of the LORD, and this is their vindication from me, declares the LORD.

Luke 4:40

When the sun was setting, the people brought to Jesus all who had various kinds of sickness, and laying his hands on each one, he healed them.

Ephesians 6:12

For our struggle is not against flesh and blood, but against the rulers, against the authorities, against the powers of this dark world and against the spiritual forces of evil in the heavenly realms.

Luke 9:11

But the crowds learned about it and followed him. He welcomed them and spoke to them about the kingdom of God, and healed those who needed healing.

Isaiah 41:10

So do not fear, for I am with you; do not be dismayed, for I am your God. I will strengthen you and help you; I will uphold you with my righteous right hand.

2 Timothy 4:18

The Lord will rescue me from every evil attack and will bring me safely to his heavenly kingdom. To him be glory for ever and ever. Amen.

Romans 8:37

No, in all these things we are more than conquerors through him who loved us.

Matthew 7:7-8

Ask and it will be given to you; seek and you will find; knock and the door will be opened to you. For everyone who asks receives; he who seeks finds; and to him who knocks, the door will be opened.

1 John 5:14-15

This is the confidence we have in approaching God: that if we ask anything according to his will, he hears us. And if we know that he hears us—whatever we ask—we know that we have what we asked of him.

Psalm 37:4-5

Delight yourself in the LORD and he will give you the desires of your heart. Commit your way to the LORD; trust in him and he will do this:

Matthew 4:24

News about him spread all over Syria, and people brought to him all who were ill with various diseases, those suffering severe pain, the demon-possessed, those having seizures, and the paralyzed, and he healed them.

Ephesians 3:20-21

Now to him who is able to do immeasurably more than all we ask or imagine, according to his power that is at work within us, to him be glory in the church and in Christ Jesus throughout all generations, for ever and ever! Amen.

John 8:32

Then you will know the truth, and the truth will set you free.

2 Corinthians 10:3-5

For though we live in the world, we do not wage war as the world does. The weapons we fight with are not the weapons of the world. On the contrary, they have divine power to demolish strongholds. We demolish arguments and every pretension that sets itself up against the knowledge of God, and we take captive every thought to make it obedient to Christ.

Matthew 9:35

Jesus went through all the towns and villages, teaching in their synagogues, preaching the good news of the kingdom and healing every disease and sickness.

James 5:15-16

And the prayer offered in faith will make the sick person well; the Lord will raise him up. If he has sinned, he will be forgiven. Therefore confess your sins to each other and pray for each other so that you may be healed. The prayer of a righteous man is powerful and effective.

John 15:7

If you remain in me and my words remain in you, ask whatever you wish, and it will be given you.

1 Peter 5:7-8

Cast all your anxiety on him because he cares for you. Be self-controlled and alert. Your enemy the devil prowls around like a roaring lion looking for someone to devour.

Acts 4:29-30

Now, Lord, consider their threats and enable your servants to speak your word with great boldness. Stretch out your hand to heal and perform miraculous signs and wonders through the name of your holy servant Jesus.

John 16:23-24

In that day you will no longer ask me anything. I tell you the truth, my Father will give you whatever you ask in my name. Until now you have not asked for anything in my name. Ask and you will receive, and your joy will be complete.

Isaiah 54:14

In righteousness you will be established: Tyranny will be far from you; you will have nothing to fear. Terror will be far removed; it will not come near you.

Marriage

1 Thessalonians 5:11

Therefore encourage one another and build each other up, just as in fact you are doing.

Romans 14:19

Let us therefore make every effort to do what leads to peace and to mutual edification.

1 Corinthians 14:26

What then shall we say, brothers? When you come together, everyone has a hymn, or a word of instruction, a revelation, a tongue or an interpretation. All of these must be done for the strengthening of the church.

1 Corinthians 7:33-34

But a married man is concerned about the affairs of this world—how he can please his wife— and his interests are divided. An unmarried woman or virgin is concerned about the Lord's affairs: Her aim is to be devoted to the Lord in both body and spirit. But a married woman is concerned about the affairs of this world—how she can please her husband.

Proverbs 31:11-16

Her husband has full confidence in her and lacks nothing of value. She brings him good, not harm, all the days of her life. She selects wool and flax and works with eager hands. She is like the merchant ships, bringing her food from afar. She gets up while it is still dark; she provides food for her family and portions for her servant girls. She considers a field and buys it; out of her earnings she plants a vineyard.

Proverbs 31:17-19

She sets about her work vigorously; her arms are strong for her tasks. She sees that her trading is profitable, and her lamp does not go out at night. In her hand she holds the distaff and grasps the spindle with her fingers.

Proverbs 31:20-25

She opens her arms to the poor and extends her hands to the needy. When it snows, she has no fear for her household; for all of them are clothed in scarlet. She makes coverings for her bed; she is clothed in fine linen and purple. Her husband is respected at the city gate, where he takes his seat among the elders of the land. She makes linen garments and sells them, and supplies the merchants with sashes. She is clothed with strength and dignity; she can laugh at the days to come.

Proverbs 31:26-29

She speaks with wisdom, and faithful instruction is on her tongue. She watches over the affairs of her household and does not eat the bread of idleness. Her children arise and call her blessed; her husband also, and he praises her: "Many women do noble things, but you surpass them all."

Proverbs 31:30-31

Charm is deceptive, and beauty is fleeting; but a woman who fears the LORD is to be praised. Give her the reward she has earned, and let her works bring her praise at the city gate.

Colossians 3:18-19

Wives, submit to your husbands, as is fitting in the Lord. Husbands, love your wives and do not be harsh with them.

Ephesians 5:21-24

Submit to one another out of reverence for Christ. Wives, submit to your husbands as to the Lord. For the husband is the head of the wife as Christ is the head of the church, his body, of which he is the Savior. Now as the church submits to Christ, so also wives should submit to their husbands in everything.

Ephesians 5:25-29

Husbands, love your wives, just as Christ loved the church and gave himself up for her to make her holy, cleansing her by the washing with water through the word, and to present her to himself as a radiant church, without stain or wrinkle or any other blemish, but holy and blameless. In this same way, husbands ought to love their wives as their own bodies. He who loves his wife loves himself. After all, no one ever hated his own body, but he feeds and cares for it, just as Christ does the church.

Ephesians 5:30-33

For we are members of his body. "For this reason a man will leave his father and mother and be united to his wife, and the two will become one flesh." This is a profound mystery—but I am talking about Christ and the church. However, each one of you also must love his wife as he loves himself, and the wife must respect her husband.

1 Corinthians 7:3

The husband should fulfill his marital duty to his wife, and likewise the wife to her husband.

1 Peter 3:7

Husbands, in the same way be considerate as you live with your wives, and treat them with respect as the weaker partner and as heirs with you of the gracious gift of life, so that nothing will hinder your prayers.

1 Peter 3:8-9

Finally, all of you, live in harmony with one another; be sympathetic, love as brothers, be compassionate and humble. Do not repay evil with evil or insult with insult, but with blessing, because to this you were called so that you may inherit a blessing.

1 Peter 3:10-12

For, "Whoever would love life and see good days must keep his tongue from evil and his lips from deceitful speech. He must turn from evil and do good; he must seek peace and pursue it. For the eyes of the Lord are on the righteous and his ears are attentive to their prayer, but the face of the Lord is against those who do evil."

1 Peter 4:8

Above all, love each other deeply, because love covers over a multitude of sins.

1 Thessalonians 5:15

Make sure that nobody pays back wrong for wrong, but always try to be kind to each other and to everyone else.

Ephesians 4:29

Do not let any unwholesome talk come out of your mouths, but only what is helpful for building others up according to their needs, that it may benefit those who listen.

Colossians 3:8-9

But now you must rid yourselves of all such things as these: anger, rage, malice, slander, and filthy language from your lips. Do not lie to each other, since you have taken off your old self with its practices.

Colossians 3:12-15

Therefore, as God's chosen people, holy and dearly loved, clothe yourselves with compassion, kindness, humility, gentleness and patience. Bear with each other and forgive whatever grievances you may have against one another. Forgive as the Lord forgave you. And over all these virtues put on love, which binds them all together in perfect unity. Let the peace of Christ rule in your hearts, since as members of one body you were called to peace. And be thankful.

Meditating on the Word

Proverbs 3:1-6

My son, do not forget my teaching, but keep my commands in your heart, for they will prolong your life many years and bring you prosperity. Let love and faithfulness never leave you; bind them around your neck, write them on the tablet of your heart. Then you will win favor and a good name in the sight of God and man. Trust in the LORD with all your heart and lean not on your own understanding; in all your ways acknowledge him, and he will make your paths straight.

Psalm 19:14

May the words of my mouth and the meditation of my heart be pleasing in your sight, O Lord, my Rock and my Redeemer.

Philippians 4:8-9

Finally, brothers, whatever is true, whatever is noble, whatever is right, whatever is pure, whatever is lovely, whatever is admirable—if anything is excellent or praiseworthy—think about such things. Whatever you have learned or received or heard from me, or seen in me—put it into practice. And the God of peace will be with you.

Psalm 19:7-9

The law of the LORD is perfect, reviving the soul. The statutes of the LORD are trustworthy, making wise the simple. The precepts of the LORD are right, giving joy to the heart. The commands of the LORD are radiant, giving light to the eyes. The fear of the LORD is pure, enduring forever. The ordinances of the LORD are sure and altogether righteous.

Psalm 119:97-98

Oh, how I love your law! I meditate on it all day long. Your commands make me wiser than my enemies, for they are ever with me.

Psalm 119:160

All your words are true; all your righteous laws are eternal.

Hebrews 4:12

For the word of God is living and active. Sharper than any double-edged sword, it penetrates even to dividing soul and spirit, joints and marrow; it judges the thoughts and attitudes of the heart.

James 1:25

But the man who looks intently into the perfect law that gives freedom, and continues to do this, not forgetting what he has heard, but doing it—he will be blessed in what he does.

1 Peter 2:2

Like newborn babies, crave pure spiritual milk, so that by it you may grow up in your salvation.

John 15:10-11

If you obey my commands, you will remain in my love, just as I have obeyed my Father's commands and remain in his love. I have told you this so that my joy may be in you and that your joy may be complete.

Luke 6:47-49

I will show you what he is like who comes to me and hears my words and puts them into practice. He is like a man building a house, who dug down deep and laid the foundation on rock. When a flood came, the torrent struck that house but could not shake it, because it was well built. But the one who hears my words and does not put them into practice is like a man who built a house on the ground without a foundation. The moment the torrent struck that house, it collapsed and its destruction was complete.

1 John 2:3-5

We know that we have come to know him if we obey his commands. The man who says, "I know him," but does not do what he commands is a liar, and the truth is not in him. But if anyone obeys his word, God's love is truly made complete in him. This is how we know we are in him.

Psalm 119:165

Great peace have they who love your law, and nothing can make them stumble.

Isaiah 48:18

If only you had paid attention to my commands, your peace would have been like a river, your righteousness like the waves of the sea.

Psalm 1:1-3

Blessed is the man who does not walk in the counsel of the wicked or stand in the way of sinners or sit in the seat of mockers. But his delight is in the law of the LORD, and on his law he meditates day and night. He is like a tree planted by streams of water, which yields its fruit in season and whose leaf does not wither. Whatever he does prospers.

Psalm 18:30-31

As for God, his way is perfect; the word of the LORD is flawless. He is a shield for all who take refuge in him. For who is God besides the LORD? And who is the Rock except our God?

John 5:24

I tell you the truth, whoever hears my word and believes him who sent me has eternal life and will not be condemned; he has crossed over from death to life.

John 8:31-32

To the Jews who had believed him, Jesus said, "If you hold to my teaching, you are really my disciples. Then you will know the truth, and the truth will set you free."

Romans 10:13

"Everyone who calls on the name of the Lord will be saved."

1 John 5:3-5

This is love for God: to obey his commands. And his commands are not burdensome, for everyone born of God overcomes the world. This is the victory that has overcome the world, even our faith. Who is it that overcomes the world? Only he who believes that Jesus is the Son of God.

John 15:7

If you remain in me and my words remain in you, ask whatever you wish, and it will be given you.

Isaiah 43:26

Review the past for me, let us argue the matter together; state the case for your innocence.

Acts 4:29-30

Now, Lord, consider their threats and enable your servants to speak your word with great boldness. Stretch out your hand to heal and perform miraculous signs and wonders through the name of your holy servant Jesus.

Jeremiah 1:12

The LORD said to me, "You have seen correctly, for I am watching to see that my word is fulfilled."

John 15:7

If you remain in me and my words remain in you, ask whatever you wish, and it will be given you.

Peace and Trust

Isaiah 54:13

All your sons will be taught by the LORD, and great will be your children's peace.

Isaiah 54:14

In righteousness you will be established: Tyranny will be far from you; you will have nothing to fear. Terror will be far removed; it will not come near you.

Psalm 29:11

The LORD gives strength to his people; the LORD blesses his people with peace.

Psalm 119:165

Great peace have they who love your law, and nothing can make them stumble.

Isaiah 48:18

If only you had paid attention to my commands, your peace would have been like a river, your righteousness like the waves of the sea.

John 14:27

Peace I leave with you; my peace I give you. I do not give to you as the world gives. Do not let your hearts be troubled and do not be afraid.

John 16:33

"I have told you these things, so that in me you may have peace. In this world you will have trouble. But take heart! I have overcome the world."

Philippians 4:6-7

Do not be anxious about anything, but in everything, by prayer and petition, with thanksgiving, present your requests to God. And the peace of God, which transcends all understanding, will guard your hearts and your minds in Christ Jesus.

Romans 5:1

Therefore, since we have been justified through faith, we have peace with God through our Lord Jesus Christ,

Psalm 34:14

Turn from evil and do good; seek peace and pursue it.

Colossians 3:15

Let the peace of Christ rule in your hearts, since as members of one body you were called to peace. And be thankful.

Psalm 57:1

(When he had fled from Saul into the cave.) Have mercy on me, O God, have mercy on me, for in you my soul takes refuge. I will take refuge in the shadow of your wings until the disaster has passed.

2 Timothy 4:18

The Lord will rescue me from every evil attack and will bring me safely to his heavenly kingdom. To him be glory for ever and ever. Amen.

1 Peter 5:7

Cast all your anxiety on him because he cares for you.

Isaiah 26:3-4

You will keep in perfect peace him whose mind is steadfast, because he trusts in you. Trust in the LORD forever, for the LORD, the LORD, is the Rock eternal.

Isaiah 54:17

No weapon forged against you will prevail, and you will refute every tongue that accuses you. This is the heritage of the servants of the LORD, and this is their vindication from me, declares the LORD.

Matthew 28:18

Then Jesus came to them and said, All authority in heaven and on earth has been given to me.

John 14:12

I tell you the truth, anyone who has faith in me will do what I have been doing. He will do even greater things than these, because I am going to the Father.

Isaiah 41:10

So do not fear, for I am with you; do not be dismayed, for I am your God. I will strengthen you and help you; I will uphold you with my righteous right hand.

Jeremiah 17:7-8

"But blessed is the man who trusts in the LORD, whose confidence is in him. He will be like a tree planted by the water that sends out its roots by the stream. It does not fear when heat comes; its leaves are always green. It has no worries in a year of drought and never fails to bear fruit."

Psalm 1:1-3

Blessed is the man who does not walk in the counsel of the wicked or stand in the way of sinners or sit in the seat of mockers. But his delight is in the law of the LORD, and on his law he meditates day and night. He is like a tree planted by streams of water, which yields its fruit in season and whose leaf does not wither. Whatever he does prospers.

John 14:1

Do not let your hearts be troubled. Trust in God; trust also in me.

Psalm 18:30-31

As for God, his way is perfect; the word of the LORD is flawless. He is a shield for all who take refuge in him. For who is God besides the LORD? And who is the Rock except our God?

Romans 15:13

May the God of hope fill you with all joy and peace as you trust in him, so that you may overflow with hope by the power of the Holy Spirit.

Proverbs 3:5-6

Trust in the LORD with all your heart and lean not on your own understanding; in all your ways acknowledge him, and he will make your paths straight.

Isaiah 54:10

Though the mountains be shaken and the hills be removed, yet my unfailing love for you will not be shaken nor my covenant of peace be removed, says the LORD, who has compassion on you.

Jeremiah 29:11-13

For I know the plans I have for you, declares the LORD, plans to prosper you and not to harm you, plans to give you hope and a future. Then you will call upon me and come and pray to me, and I will listen to you. You will seek me and find me when you seek me with all your heart.

John 16:23-24

In that day you will no longer ask me anything. I tell you the truth, my Father will give you whatever you ask in my name. Until now you have not asked for anything in my name. Ask and you will receive, and your joy will be complete.

1 John 5:14-15

This is the confidence we have in approaching God: that if we ask anything according to his will, he hears us. And if we know that he hears us—whatever we ask—we know that we have what we asked of him.

Psalm 23:1-6

The LORD is my shepherd, I shall not be in want. He makes me lie down in green pastures, he leads me beside quiet waters, he restores my soul. He guides me in paths of righteousness for his name's sake. Even though I walk through the valley of the shadow of death, I will fear no evil, for you are with me; your rod and your staff, they comfort me. You prepare a table before me in the presence of my enemies. You anoint my head with oil; my cup overflows. Surely goodness and love will follow me all the days of my life, and I will dwell in the house of the LORD forever.

Prayer and Faith

Isaiah 55:6-9

Seek the LORD while he may be found; call on him while he is near. Let the wicked forsake his way and the evil man his thoughts. Let him turn to the LORD, and he will have mercy on him, and to our God, for he will freely pardon. "For my thoughts are not your thoughts, neither are your ways my ways," declares the LORD. "As the heavens are higher than the earth, so are my ways higher than your ways and my thoughts than your thoughts.

Isaiah 55:10-13

As the rain and the snow come down from heaven, and do not return to it without watering the earth and making it bud and flourish, so that it yields seed for the sower and bread for the eater, so is my word that goes out from my mouth: It will not return to me empty, but will accomplish what I desire and achieve the purpose for which I sent it. You will go out in joy and be led forth in peace; the mountains and hills will burst into song before you, and all the trees of the field will clap their hands. Instead of the thornbush will grow the pine tree, and instead of briers the myrtle will grow. This will be for the LORD's renown, for an everlasting sign, which will not be destroyed.

Psalm 126:5-6

Those who sow in tears will reap with songs of joy. He who goes out weeping, carrying seed to sow, will return with songs of joy, carrying sheaves with him.

Psalm 37:4-5

Delight yourself in the LORD and he will give you the desires of your heart. Commit your way to the LORD; trust in him and he will do this.

Ephesians 3:20-21

Now to him who is able to do immeasurably more than all we ask or imagine, according to his power that is at work within us, to him be glory in the church and in Christ Jesus throughout all generations, for ever and ever! Amen.

Matthew 21:21-22

Jesus replied, "I tell you the truth, if you have faith and do not doubt, not only can you do what was done to the fig tree, but also you can say to this mountain, 'Go, throw yourself into the sea,' and it will be done. If you believe, you will receive whatever you ask for in prayer."

Matthew 8:13

Then Jesus said to the centurion, "Go! It will be done just as you believed it would." And his servant was healed at that very hour.

Mark 9:23

"'If you can'?" said Jesus. "Everything is possible for him who believes."

Matthew 17:20-21

He replied, "Because you have so little faith. I tell you the truth, if you have faith as small as a mustard seed, you can say to this mountain, 'Move from here to there' and it will move. Nothing will be impossible for you."

Luke 8:48

Then he said to her, "Daughter, your faith has healed you. Go in peace."

Luke 8:50

Hearing this, Jesus said to Jairus, "Don't be afraid; just believe, and she will be healed."

Hebrews 11:1

Now faith is being sure of what we hope for and certain of what we do not see.

Mark 11:23

I tell you the truth, if anyone says to this mountain, 'Go, throw yourself into the sea,' and does not doubt in his heart but believes that what he says will happen, it will be done for him.

Mark 11:24-26

Therefore I tell you, whatever you ask for in prayer, believe that you have received it, and it will be yours. And when you stand praying, if you hold anything against anyone, forgive him, so that your Father in heaven may forgive you your sins.

Matthew 9:29

Then he touched their eyes and said, "According to your faith will it be done to you."

Acts 27:25

So keep up your courage, men, for I have faith in God that it will happen just as he told me.

Ephesians 3:11-12

According to his eternal purpose which he accomplished in Christ Jesus our Lord. In him and through faith in him we may approach God with freedom and confidence.

Jeremiah 29:11-13

For I know the plans I have for you, declares the LORD, plans to prosper you and not to harm you, plans to give you hope and a future. Then you will call upon me and come and pray to me, and I will listen to you. You will seek me and find me when you seek me with all your heart.

Romans 10:17

Consequently, faith comes from hearing the message, and the message is heard through the word of Christ.

Luke 17:6

He replied, If you have faith as small as a mustard seed, you can say to this mulberry tree, 'Be uprooted and planted in the sea,' and it will obey you.

Romans 1:17

For in the gospel a righteousness from God is revealed, a righteousness that is by faith from first to last, just as it is written: "The righteous will live by faith."

Galatians 5:22-23

But the fruit of the Spirit is love, joy, peace, patience, kindness, goodness, faithfulness, gentleness and self-control. Against such things there is no law.

Hebrews 12:1-2

Therefore, since we are surrounded by such a great cloud of witnesses, let us throw off everything that hinders and the sin that so easily entangles, and let us run with perseverance the race marked out for us. Let us fix our eyes on Jesus, the author and perfecter of our faith, who for the joy set before him endured the cross, scorning its shame, and sat down at the right hand of the throne of God.

James 5:15-16

And the prayer offered in faith will make the sick person well; the Lord will raise him up. If he has sinned, he will be forgiven. Therefore confess your sins to each other and pray for each other so that you may be healed. The prayer of a righteous man is powerful and effective.

Protection from Danger

Psalm 91:1-3

He who dwells in the shelter of the Most High will rest in the shadow of the Almighty. I will say of the LORD, "He is my refuge and my fortress, my God, in whom I trust." Surely he will save you from the fowler's snare and from the deadly pestilence.

Psalm 91:4-7

He will cover you with his feathers, and under his wings you will find refuge; his faithfulness will be your shield and rampart. You will not fear the terror of night, nor the arrow that flies by day, nor the pestilence that stalks in the darkness, nor the plague that destroys at midday. A thousand may fall at your side, ten thousand at your right hand, but it will not come near you.

Psalm 91:9-10

If you make the Most High your dwelling- even the LORD, who is my refuge- then no harm will befall you, no disaster will come near your tent.

Psalm 91:11-12

For he will command his angels concerning you to guard you in all your ways; they will lift you up in their hands, so that you will not strike your foot against a stone.

Psalm 91:13-14

You will tread upon the lion and the cobra; you will trample the great lion and the serpent. "Because he loves me," says the LORD, "I will rescue him; I will protect him, for he acknowledges my name.

Psalm 91:15-16

He will call upon me, and I will answer him; I will be with him in trouble, I will deliver him and honor him. With long life will I satisfy him and show him my salvation."

Luke 10:19-20

I have given you authority to trample on snakes and scorpions and to overcome all the power of the enemy; nothing will harm you. However, do not rejoice that the spirits submit to you, but rejoice that your names are written in heaven."

Deuteronomy 20:1-4

When you go to war against your enemies and see horses and chariots and an army greater than yours, do not be afraid of them, because the LORD your God, who brought you up out of Egypt, will be with you. When you are about to go into battle, the priest shall come forward and address the army. He shall say: "Hear, O Israel, today you are going into battle against your enemies. Do not be fainthearted or afraid; do not be terrified or give way to panic before them. For the LORD your God is the one who goes with you to fight for you against your enemies to give you victory."

Psalm 138:7

Though I walk in the midst of trouble, you preserve my life; you stretch out your hand against the anger of my foes, with your right hand you save me.

Isaiah 43:1-2

But now, this is what the LORD says- he who created you, O Jacob, he who formed you, O Israel: Fear not, for I have redeemed you; I have summoned you by name; you are mine. When you pass through the waters, I will be with you; and when you pass through the rivers, they will not sweep over you. When you walk through the fire, you will not be burned; the flames will not set you ablaze.

Romans 8:31

What, then, shall we say in response to this? If God is for us, who can be against us?

Isaiah 54:14

In righteousness you will be established: Tyranny will be far from you; you will have nothing to fear. Terror will be far removed; it will not come near you.

Psalm 46:1

God is our refuge and strength, an ever-present help in trouble.

Romans 8:37

No, in all these things we are more than conquerors through him who loved us.

Psalm 3:3

But you are a shield around me, O LORD; you bestow glory on me and lift up my head.

2 Thessalonians 3:2-3

And pray that we may be delivered from wicked and evil men, for not everyone has faith. But the Lord is faithful, and he will strengthen and protect you from the evil one.

Psalm 116:1-2

I love the LORD, for he heard my voice; he heard my cry for mercy. Because he turned his ear to me, I will call on him as long as I live.

Psalm 34:7

The angel of the LORD encamps around those who fear him, and he delivers them.

2 Corinthians 10:3-5

For though we live in the world, we do not wage war as the world does. The weapons we fight with are not the weapons of the world. On the contrary, they have divine power to demolish strongholds. We demolish arguments and every pretension that sets itself up against the knowledge of God, and we take captive every thought to make it obedient to Christ.

Mark 11:22-24

"Have faith in God," Jesus answered. I tell you the truth, if anyone says to this mountain, 'Go, throw yourself into the sea,' and does not doubt in his heart but believes that what he says will happen, it will be done for him. Therefore I tell you, whatever you ask for in prayer, believe that you have received it, and it will be yours.

1 John 5:3-5

This is love for God: to obey his commands. And his commands are not burdensome, for everyone born of God overcomes the world. This is the victory that has overcome the world, even our faith. Who is it that overcomes the world? Only he who believes that Jesus is the Son of God.

John 8:36

So if the Son sets you free, you will be free indeed.

1 Peter 5:7-8

Cast all your anxiety on him because he cares for you. Be self-controlled and alert. Your enemy the devil prowls around like a roaring lion looking for someone to devour.

Acts 4:29-30

Now, Lord, consider their threats and enable your servants to speak your word with great boldness. Stretch out your hand to heal and perform miraculous signs and wonders through the name of your holy servant Jesus.

John 16:23-24

In that day you will no longer ask me anything. I tell you the truth, my Father will give you whatever you ask in my name. Until now you have not asked for anything in my name. Ask and you will receive, and your joy will be complete.

1 John 5:14-15

This is the confidence we have in approaching God: that if we ask anything according to his will, he hears us. And if we know that he hears us—whatever we ask—we know that we have what we asked of him.

Financial Provision

Psalm 23:5

You prepare a table before me in the presence of my enemies. You anoint my head with oil; my cup overflows.

Malachi 3:10-12

Bring the whole tithe into the storehouse, that there may be food in my house. Test me in this, says the LORD Almighty, "and see if I will not throw open the floodgates of heaven and pour out so much blessing that you will not have room enough for it. I will prevent pests from devouring your crops, and the vines in your fields will not cast their fruit," says the LORD Almighty. "Then all the nations will call you blessed, for yours will be a delightful land," says the LORD Almighty.

Philippians 4:19

And my God will meet all your needs according to his glorious riches in Christ Jesus.

Luke 6:38

Give, and it will be given to you. A good measure, pressed down, shaken together and running over, will be poured into your lap. For with the measure you use, it will be measured to you.

Isaiah 61:3

And provide for those who grieve in Zion- to bestow on them a crown of beauty instead of ashes, the oil of gladness instead of mourning, and a garment of praise instead of a spirit of despair. They will be called oaks of righteousness, a planting of the LORD for the display of his splendor.

Ephesians 4:28

He who has been stealing must steal no longer, but must work, doing something useful with his own hands, that he may have something to share with those in need.

Matthew 6:33

But seek first his kingdom and his righteousness, and all these things will be given to you as well.

2 Corinthians 9:6-7

Remember this: Whoever sows sparingly will also reap sparingly, and whoever sows generously will also reap generously. Each man should give what he has decided in his heart to give, not reluctantly or under compulsion, for God loves a cheerful giver.

2 Corinthians 9:8

And God is able to make all grace abound to you, so that in all things at all times, having all that you need, you will abound in every good work.

Galatians 3:13

Christ redeemed us from the curse of the law by becoming a curse for us, for it is written: "Cursed is everyone who is hung on a tree."

Joel 2:25-26

I will repay you for the years the locusts have eaten- the great locust and the young locust, the other locusts and the locust swarm - my great army that I sent among you. You will have plenty to eat, until you are full, and you will praise the name of the LORD your God, who has worked wonders for you; never again will my people be shamed.

2 Corinthians 8:9

For you know the grace of our Lord Jesus Christ, that though he was rich, yet for your sakes he became poor, so that you through his poverty might become rich.

3 John 2

Dear friend, I pray that you may enjoy good health and that all may go well with you, even as your soul is getting along well.

Proverbs 3:9-10

Honor the LORD with your wealth, with the firstfruits of all your crops; then your barns will be filled to overflowing, and your vats will brim over with new wine.

Proverbs 22:4

Humility and the fear of the LORD bring wealth and honor and life.

Proverbs 22:9

A generous man will himself be blessed, for he shares his food with the poor.

Proverbs 28:19

He who works his land will have abundant food, but the one who chases fantasies will have his fill of poverty.

Proverbs 28:27

He who gives to the poor will lack nothing, but he who closes his eyes to them receives many curses.

Deuteronomy 28:1-6

If you fully obey the LORD your God and carefully follow all his commands I give you today, the LORD your God will set you high above all the nations on earth. All these blessings will come upon you and accompany you if you obey the LORD your God: You will be blessed in the city and blessed in the country. The fruit of your womb will be blessed, and the crops of your land and the young of your livestock-the calves of your herds and the lambs of your flocks. Your basket and your kneading trough will be blessed. You will be blessed when you come in and blessed when you go out.

Deuteronomy 28:7

The LORD will grant that the enemies who rise up against you will be defeated before you. They will come at you from one direction but flee from you in seven.

Deuteronomy 28:8

The LORD will send a blessing on your barns and on everything you put your hand to. The LORD your God will bless you in the land he is giving you.

Deuteronomy 28:9-10

The LORD will establish you as his holy people, as he promised you on oath, if you keep the commands of the LORD your God and walk in his ways. Then all the peoples on earth will see that you are called by the name of the LORD, and they will fear you.

Deuteronomy 28:11-12

The LORD will grant you abundant prosperity-in the fruit of your womb, the young of your livestock and the crops of your ground-in the land he swore to your forefathers to give you. The LORD will open the heavens, the storehouse of his bounty, to send rain on your land in season and to bless all the work of your hands. You will lend to many nations but will borrow from none.

Deuteronomy 28:13

The LORD will make you the head, not the tail. If you pay attention to the commands of the LORD your God that I give you this day and carefully follow them, you will always be at the top, never at the bottom.

Deuteronomy 8:18

But remember the LORD your God, for it is he who gives you the ability to produce wealth, and so confirms his covenant, which he swore to your forefathers, as it is today.

Psalm 37:4-5

Delight yourself in the LORD and he will give you the desires of your heart. Commit your way to the LORD; trust in him and he will do this.

Matthew 21:22

If you believe, you will receive whatever you ask for in prayer.

Mark 11:22-24

"Have faith in God," Jesus answered. "I tell you the truth, if anyone says to this mountain, 'Go, throw yourself into the sea,' and does not doubt in his heart but believes that what he says will happen, it will be done for him. Therefore I tell you, whatever you ask for in prayer, believe that you have received it, and it will be yours.

John 15:7

If you remain in me and my words remain in you, ask whatever you wish, and it will be given you.

James 5:16

Therefore confess your sins to each other and pray for each other so that you may be healed. The prayer of a righteous man is powerful and effective.

John 16:23-24

In that day you will no longer ask me anything. I tell you the truth, my Father will give you whatever you ask in my name. Until now you have not asked for anything in my name. Ask and you will receive, and your joy will be complete.

1 John 5:14-15

This is the confidence we have in approaching God: that if we ask anything according to his will, he hears us. And if we know that he hears us—whatever we ask—we know that we have what we asked of him.

Jeremiah 1:12

The LORD said to me, "You have seen correctly, for I am watching to see that my word is fulfilled."

Isaiah 54:14

In righteousness you will be established: Tyranny will be far from you; you will have nothing to fear. Terror will be far removed; it will not come near you.

Salvation in Jesus

2 Peter 3:9

The Lord is not slow in keeping his promise, as some understand slowness. He is patient with you, not wanting anyone to perish, but everyone to come to repentance.

2 Corinthians 6:2

For he says, "In the time of my favor I heard you, and in the day of salvation I helped you." I tell you, now is the time of God's favor, now is the day of salvation.

Revelation 3:20

Here I am! I stand at the door and knock. If anyone hears my voice and opens the door, I will come in and eat with him, and he with me.

2 Corinthians 4:3-4

The god of this age has blinded the minds of unbelievers, so that they cannot see the light of the gospel of the glory of Christ, who is the image of God.

Luke 9:23-24

Then he said to them all: "If anyone would come after me, he must deny himself and take up his cross daily and follow me. For whoever wants to save his life will lose it, but whoever loses his life for me will save it.

Romans 10:13

"Everyone who calls on the name of the Lord will be saved."

Mark 16:16

Whoever believes and is baptized will be saved, but whoever does not believe will be condemned.

2 Corinthians 5:17

Therefore, if anyone is in Christ, he is a new creation; the old has gone, the new has come!

Isaiah 43:25

I, even I, am he who blots out your transgressions, for my own sake, and remembers your sins no more.

Colossians 2:13-15

When you were dead in your sins and in the uncircumcision of your sinful nature, God made you alive with Christ. He forgave us all our sins, having canceled the written code, with its regulations, that was against us and that stood opposed to us; he took it away, nailing it to the cross. And having disarmed the powers and authorities, he made a public spectacle of them, triumphing over them by the cross.

Isaiah 1:18

"Come now, let us reason together," says the LORD. Though your sins are like scarlet, they shall be as white as snow; though they are red as crimson, they shall be like wool.

Psalm 32:1-2

Blessed is he whose transgressions are forgiven, whose sins are covered. Blessed is the man whose sin the LORD does not count against him and in whose spirit is no deceit.

1 John 1:8-9

If we claim to be without sin, we deceive ourselves and the truth is not in us. If we confess our sins, he is faithful and just and will forgive us our sins and purify us from all unrighteousness.

Ephesians 1:6-7

To the praise of his glorious grace, which he has freely given us in the One he loves. In him we have redemption through his blood, the forgiveness of sins, in accordance with the riches of God's grace.

John 3:16-17

For God so loved the world that he gave his one and only Son, that whoever believes in him shall not perish but have eternal life. For God did not send his Son into the world to condemn the world, but to save the world through him.

Romans 10:9-10

That if you confess with your mouth, "Jesus is Lord," and believe in your heart that God raised him from the dead, you will be saved. For it is with your heart that you believe and are justified, and it is with your mouth that you confess and are saved.

1 John 4:13-15

We know that we live in him and he in us, because he has given us of his Spirit. And we have seen and testify that the Father has sent his Son to be the Savior of the world. If anyone acknowledges that Jesus is the Son of God, God lives in him and he in God.

Philippians 2:9-11

Therefore God exalted him to the highest place and gave him the name that is above every name, that at the name of Jesus every knee should bow, in heaven and on earth and under the earth, and every tongue confess that Jesus Christ is Lord, to the glory of God the Father.

Romans 6:23

For the wages of sin is death, but the gift of God is eternal life in Christ Jesus our Lord.

John 11:25-26

Jesus said to her, "I am the resurrection and the life. He who believes in me will live, even though he dies; and whoever lives and believes in me will never die. Do you believe this?"

John 5:24

I tell you the truth, whoever hears my word and believes him who sent me has eternal life and will not be condemned; he has crossed over from death to life.

Ephesians 2:8-9

For it is by grace you have been saved, through faith—and this not from yourselves, it is the gift of God— not by works, so that no one can boast.

Hebrews 12:1-2

Therefore, since we are surrounded by such a great cloud of witnesses, let us throw off everything that hinders and the sin that so easily entangles, and let us run with perseverance the race marked out for us. Let us fix our eyes on Jesus, the author and perfecter of our faith, who for the joy set before him endured the cross, scorning its shame, and sat down at the right hand of the throne of God.

Sleep

Proverbs 3:24

When you lie down, you will not be afraid; when you lie down, your sleep will be sweet.

Isaiah 41:10

So do not fear, for I am with you; do not be dismayed, for I am your God. I will strengthen you and help you; I will uphold you with my righteous right hand.

John 14:27

Peace I leave with you; my peace I give you. I do not give to you as the world gives. Do not let your hearts be troubled and do not be afraid.

Leviticus 26:6

I will grant peace in the land, and you will lie down and no one will make you afraid. I will remove savage beasts from the land, and the sword will not pass through your country.

Psalm 23:1-6

The LORD is my shepherd, I shall not be in want. He makes me lie down in green pastures, he leads me beside quiet waters, he restores my soul. He guides me in paths of righteousness for his name's sake. Even though I walk through the valley of the shadow of death, I will fear no evil, for you are with me; your rod and your staff, they comfort me. You prepare a table before me in the presence of my enemies. You anoint my head with oil; my cup overflows. Surely goodness and love will follow me all the days of my life, and I will dwell in the house of the LORD forever.

Psalm 4:8

I will lie down and sleep in peace, for you alone, O LORD, make me dwell in safety.

Ecclesiastes 5:12

The sleep of a laborer is sweet, whether he eats little or much, but the abundance of a rich man permits him no sleep.

Psalm 3:3-5

But you are a shield around me, O LORD; you bestow glory on me and lift up my head. To the LORD I cry aloud, and he answers me from his holy hill. Selah. I lie down and sleep; I wake again, because the LORD sustains me.

Psalm 91:5-7

You will not fear the terror of night, nor the arrow that flies by day, nor the pestilence that stalks in the darkness, nor the plague that destroys at midday. A thousand may fall at your side, ten thousand at your right hand, but it will not come near you.

Isaiah 54:14

In righteousness you will be established: Tyranny will be far from you; you will have nothing to fear. Terror will be far removed; it will not come near you.

Treatment of Others

1 Thessalonians 5:15

Make sure that nobody pays back wrong for wrong, but always try to be kind to each other and to everyone else.

Romans 14:10

You, then, why do you judge your brother? Or why do you look down on your brother? For we will all stand before God's judgment seat.

Psalm 15:1-3

LORD, who may dwell in your sanctuary? Who may live on your holy hill? He whose walk is blameless and who does what is righteous, who speaks the truth from his heart and has no slander on his tongue, who does his neighbor no wrong and casts no slur on his fellowman.

Psalm 34:14

Turn from evil and do good; seek peace and pursue it.

Colossians 3:16-17

Let the word of Christ dwell in you richly as you teach and admonish one another with all wisdom, and as you sing psalms, hymns and spiritual songs with gratitude in your hearts to God. And whatever you do, whether in word or deed, do it all in the name of the Lord Jesus, giving thanks to God the Father through him.

Ephesians 4:29

Do not let any unwholesome talk come out of your mouths, but only what is helpful for building others up according to their needs, that it may benefit those who listen.

Colossians 3:8-9

But now you must rid yourselves of all such things as these: anger, rage, malice, slander, and filthy language from your lips. Do not lie to each other, since you have taken off your old self with its practices.

Colossians 3:12-15

Therefore, as God's chosen people, holy and dearly loved, clothe yourselves with compassion, kindness, humility, gentleness and patience. Bear with each other and forgive whatever grievances you may have against one another. Forgive as the Lord forgave you. And over all these virtues put on love, which binds them all together in perfect unity. Let the peace of Christ rule in your hearts, since as members of one body you were called to peace. And be thankful.

1 Thessalonians 5:11

Therefore encourage one another and build each other up, just as in fact you are doing.

Romans 14:19

Let us therefore make every effort to do what leads to peace and to mutual edification.

1 Corinthians 14:26

What then shall we say, brothers? When you come together, everyone has a hymn, or a word of instruction, a revelation, a tongue or an interpretation. All of these must be done for the strengthening of the church.

1 Peter 3:8-9

Finally, all of you, live in harmony with one another; be sympathetic, love as brothers, be compassionate and humble. Do not repay evil with evil or insult with insult, but with blessing, because to this you were called so that you may inherit a blessing.

Romans 12:17-18

Do not repay anyone evil for evil. Be careful to do what is right in the eyes of everybody. If it is possible, as far as it depends on you, live at peace with everyone.

Luke 6:27-28

But I tell you who hear me: Love your enemies, do good to those who hate you, bless those who curse you, pray for those who mistreat you.

2 Corinthians 13:11

Finally, brothers, good-bye. Aim for perfection, listen to my appeal, be of one mind, live in peace. And the God of love and peace will be with you.

Matthew 5:9

Blessed are the peacemakers, for they will be called sons of God.

Galatians 5:13-14

You, my brothers, were called to be free. But do not use your freedom to indulge the sinful nature; rather, serve one another in love. The entire law is summed up in a single command: "Love your neighbor as yourself."

1 Peter 5:5

Young men, in the same way be submissive to those who are older. All of you, clothe yourselves with humility toward one another, because, "God opposes the proud but gives grace to the humble."

Deuteronomy 15:7-8

If there is a poor man among your brothers in any of the towns of the land that the LORD your God is giving you, do not be hardhearted or tightfisted toward your poor brother. Rather be openhanded and freely lend him whatever he needs.

James 1:27

Religion that God our Father accepts as pure and faultless is this: to look after orphans and widows in their distress and to keep oneself from being polluted by the world.

James 2:15-16

Suppose a brother or sister is without clothes and daily food. If one of you says to him, "Go, I wish you well; keep warm and well fed," but does nothing about his physical needs, what good is it?

Mark 11:25

And when you stand praying, if you hold anything against anyone, forgive him, so that your Father in heaven may forgive you your sins.

Ephesians 4:32

Be kind and compassionate to one another, forgiving each other, just as in Christ God forgave you.

Hebrews 13:1-3

Keep on loving each other as brothers. Do not forget to entertain strangers, for by so doing some people have entertained angels without knowing it. Remember those in prison as if you were their fellow prisoners, and those who are mistreated as if you yourselves were suffering.

Matthew 10:42

And if anyone gives even a cup of cold water to one of these little ones because he is my disciple, I tell you the truth, he will certainly not lose his reward.

Matthew 5:44-45

But I tell you: Love your enemies and pray for those who persecute you, that you may be sons of your Father in heaven. He causes his sun to rise on the evil and the good, and sends rain on the righteous and the unrighteous.

John 15:13

Greater love has no one than this, that he lay down his life for his friends.

1 John 3:16

This is how we know what love is: Jesus Christ laid down his life for us. And we ought to lay down our lives for our brothers.

About the Author

Chuck Strohm has a passion for serving people, and he uses his training as a successful engineer to deconstruct concepts of faith and prayer in his book Prayer Demystified.

Chuck was elected to the Oklahoma Legislature in 2014 as a self-defined Constitutional Conservative on a platform of limited government and personal freedoms, thanks to the support of a grassroots movement. When elected, he was the only practicing engineer in the Oklahoma House of Representatives.

Chuck has served his community in a number of capacities, but his family has always come first. He and his wife, Angela, have four beautiful children—Tamara, Brittany, Andre, and Reagan. Chuck and his family are very active in their local churches and live in the Tulsa, Oklahoma, area.

If your life has been impacted by Prayer Demystified, please email us and share your testimony with us.

prayerdemystified@gmail.com